A Book of English Belief

A Book of
English Belief

Bede to Temple

Chosen by Joanna M. Hughes

SCM PRESS
London

TRINITY PRESS INTERNATIONAL
Philadelphia

First printed for private circulation in 1987
by the University Printing House, Oxford,
with help from the West African Examinations Council

This edition published 1989
Second impression 1991

SCM Press
26-30 Tottenham Road
London N1 4BZ

Trinity Press International
3725 Chestnut Street
Philadelphia PA 19104

British Library Cataloguing in Publication Data

Hughes, Joanna M.
A Book of English Belief: Bede to Temple
1. England. Christians–Biographies–Collections
I.Title
242

ISBN 0–334–00115 3

Library of Congress Cataloging-in-Publication Data

Hughes, Joanna M.
A Book of English Belief: Bede to Temple/
edited by Joanna M. Hughes
p. cm.
Includes bibliographical references.
ISBN 0–334–00115–3
1. Christian literature, English–England. I. Hughes, Joanna M.
BR53.B66   1989   89–20174
274'.2–dc20

Photoset at The Spartan Press Ltd, Lymington, Hants
and printed in England by
Clays Ltd, St Ives plc

CONTENTS

PREFACE

Joanna Mary Hughes was among the most remarkable people I met at Oxford, probably the one who influenced me most though she was not aware of it. We met by chance in the fifties when we were both reading modern history, she at Lady Margaret Hall and I at Balliol.

She taught me to understand English history from within, not just to analyse it from without. She explored church interiors, investigated family genealogies and relationships, and read forgotten sermons that were the clues to past English thought and feeling. Through her I began to become part of the subject I was studying.

I only met her father three times. He was a scholar and a Housemaster at Rugby and 'Janny' ascribed her perception to him. After she came down from Oxford, her parents presented her with a life subscription to The London Library. She visited it regularly, often every week, and her small flat overflowing with biographies, memoirs and letters seemed an extension of it, sharing the same learned and workmanlike atmosphere.

To communicate religious history and a way of spirituality on a deep level, the teacher must embody it, incarnate it so to speak. Because she did so without being aware of it, I accepted her influence readily. It was genuine.

When I met her I had just rediscovered religion. I had lost my childhood familiarity with it, and coming to it anew, I was especially attracted to spirituality of the flashier sort – happenings, higher mysticism, indeed anything brightly coloured.

Her religion was not something she had 'taken up', but part of her nature and its characteristic was integrity, a quality outside fashion. This integrity was fundamental to her scholarship, her religion and her friendships. She had a sharp intellect, only controlled by her modesty and her sense of fairness. When she had sorted out the pompous, the pretentious and the false, she gave unstintingly to any who were weak or in need. It was lies she could not abide, no matter how pious or politic. The truth made her free of fashionable prejudice.

The reader of this book will notice its 'protestant catholicity'. Religion is for everyone. It is not a private (and all male) club for professionals. Its witnesses are politicians, parsons, society women, writers, rakes, queens, kings, poor people and tradesmen – indeed all those Englishwomen and men who tried unostentatiously to be true, stumbled and tried again. She could discern what was extra-ordinary in ordinary folk.

And folk trusted her, Jew and Gentile, English, commonwealth and foreign. Her special affection was for the academics and students of West Africa. She gave herself to them unstintingly and they gave her their trust, which she valued above all.

In the last year of her life, I suggested to her the composition of this book. I have shown the result to rabbinical students, to businessmen, to friends who believe and to those who don't. To all of them it is a window into English religion at its truest. She would have regarded such a claim as 'over the top' and exclaimed 'tush', a word I had read but never heard. In this I am content to differ.

Rabbi Lionel Blue

To the memory of my grandfather
William Francis Sorsbie and
my grandmother Blanche Sorsbie

INTRODUCTION

There are many anthologies of writing on spiritual matters, designed to entice the reader towards studying the great originals, also collections of prayers and of religious poetry.

This book is an attempt at a different task: to make an anthology from words English Christians have spoken or written during their ordinary lives or in moments of crisis rather than from their formal pronouncements on religion. It aims to show the biographical and spontaneous elements in English belief.

Limitations of space have meant confining the book to England. No attempt has been made to cover Scotland, Wales or Ireland because their deeply interesting religious histories are so entirely different from that of England; nor has anything been included concerning English missionary endeavours overseas. (But kings and queens of England have been regarded as English, even if born in Falaise or The Hague, likewise Archbishops and Prime Ministers, however Scots.)

The choice of who is included and who is omitted may surprise readers; it is a matter of intention and balance. The intention has been to show the greatest variety of characters voicing their own experience directly. For example, Shakespeare's views on religion can be studied in many places in his work, but there are no personal letters or recorded exclamations by him that could be inserted here. So, in several cases, to get the flavour of a man or woman's character, it would be necessary to turn to their formal work, because it may give the clearest picture of their views or because little or nothing personal has survived. Some such passages have been included (such as Chaucer on the country parson) but the aim has been to find extracts illustrating the direct experience of as many characters as possible, rather than to insert well-known worthies at all costs. Immediacy, not literary merit, has been the criterion for inclusion here. Therefore, the great sequence of English devotional and theological works are represented only by some very short quotations, which also help to set the scene for different periods. Some extracts from sermons creep in, as our ancestors had a great appetite for them and they can include some remarks of great shrewdness.

Religious poetry presents a difficulty, as there is so much in English of such superlative quality – English is surpassed only by Hebrew in the range of religious works of poetic genius. Only a very few examples have been included here; usually because they express some experiences more concisely than any prose.

Balance amongst entries is difficult – for example, the seventeenth and nineteenth centuries tend to take more than their fair share of space on account of those times' overwhelming interest in religion and because of the survival of so much material in comparison with earlier years. Choice from the sixteenth century is perplexing, as so many of the heartfelt words recorded were spoken during persecution – often actually at the point of death. Four hundred years later the description of Catholic martyrdoms under Henry VIII and Elizabeth I and of Protestant martyrdoms under Mary are still harrowing; the aim here has been to find less painful accounts to set beside the grievous ones.

It is hoped that the brief biographical notes will not seem unnecessary or obtrusive: short descriptions of the characters speaking may be useful, particularly because of the unexpected attitudes of many of the people quoted – for example, the revelation of self-doubt and humility by several outwardly armoured and successful men and women. It is not possible to supply biographical information about those unknown people whose voices are heard from time to time in English life: Lollards, the Puritan women of the seventeenth-century, the rank and file of the New Model Army, the early Quakers and nineteenth-century radicals. They represent the many faithful men and women throughout the centuries whose prayers have been unrecorded by everyone except God, but who have supported the life of belief in spite of every weight laid on them by the hard circumstances of their lives.

The book ends in 1944, the year of William Temple's death. The period since then has been one of experimentation in the churches – changes in organization, customs, education and liturgy. It seemed best to stop before the period of Vatican II or the union between Presbyterians and Congregationalists, rather than skimp an era of such importance.

To avoid confusion, Christians recognizing the authority of the Pope have been called Catholics and the rest Protestants. (This is an oversimplification, but saves lengthy explanatory phrasing.)

Truth and sincerity come from the past with startling immediacy, sometimes with alarming immediacy. Often it is the briefest phrases which stick in the mind: Lady Jane Grey, aged sixteen, writing shortly before her execution to her youngest sister about the Bible – 'It will teach you to live and learn you to die.'

Words from the past can feed our religion, and they can show also how much of what we mistakenly think is new has been repeated century by century. (Elizabeth I and Archbishop Benson three hundred years later both complained of the ignorance and presumption of Anglican ordinands; Lord Melbourne and Neville Chamberlain both complained of the clergy's getting involved in government policies which were none of their business.)

Collecting material from many sources provokes thought about the different themes which recur again and again in English religion. Many of them are very chastening to the self-complacency of the 1980s. For example, there is the division between the idea of the church covering the whole nation and providing for everyone and that of a gathered church of witnesses. Such powerful advocates as Archbishops Parker and Tait on the one hand and the Congregationalists Dr Owen and Dr Dale on the other, show what convincing arguments can be brought up for either view. There is the noticeable fact that for the ministry of any Christian church to flourish at its best in England there must be a religiously involved laity with a large learned element: the sixteenth-century clergy felt they had the eye of Lord Burghley upon them, those of the nineteenth that of Mr Gladstone. And the great seventeenth-century exponents of the spiritual life among the clergy grew up against a background of laity who were all – Anglican, Independent, Presbyterian, Quaker, Fifth Monarchy and Socinian – soaked through and through with the words of the Bible.

This is part of another strand of English religion, perhaps the greatest and most important; that of the primacy of the Bible in English religion. Because of the combativeness of the English temperament it has been used as a weapon as well as a light – as a weapon by laity against clergy and by clergy against laity within individual churches (St Thomas à Becket was very free with biblical references against Henry II, just as the sympathizers with Erasmus were against the keepers of shrines). The Bible has been used by one denomination against another; Charles I was as well equipped for exegesis as his Presbyterian and Independent opponents. The seventeenth-century Jesuits were as nimble as their enemies in discharging a barrage of texts; nineteenth-century Evangelicals and Tractarians, otherwise at daggers drawn, united to attack biblical critics. Sometimes, looking at the history of religion in this country, one is tempted to remark that the first thing an English Christian does with a Bible is to bang someone else over the head with it. But this militancy is, after all, a witness to a passionate attachment, to a supreme value set on what the Coronation service calls 'the lively Oracles of God'. There is nothing lukewarm in traditional English attitudes to the Bible, they burn in the spirituality of every church.

An illustration of this is the recurring tension in English spirituality between the influence of the story of Abraham and Isaac (the concept of resignation and submission to God) and the influence of the story of Jacob's struggle with the angel (the concept of wrestling with God, which is central to Puritan devotion). Sometimes people fall definitely into one or other of the categories: Queen Mary II into the first, Oliver Cromwell into the second. But often the two ways of prayer mingle in the same person, pulling for mastery.

Another result of English belief is the extraordinary capacity of thousands of people, known and unknown, for sacrifice. Not only the great martyrdoms, but other surrenders: St Augustine, who hated the thought of coming to Anglo-Saxon England to convert us; the London merchants of the 1520s who risked everything to smuggle in the first printed New Testaments in English; the young Catholic girls who for three centuries left not only home, but country too, to fulfil their vocations in the religious life; the Anglican clergy who were expelled from their parishes in the 1640s and the

Freechurchmen who were expelled from theirs in the 1660s, and so on and so on in a constant story of generous courage.

Spontaneous words can reveal the variety of Christian character and can show how God the Holy Spirit works in such different natures.

Much help in collecting material came from family and friends and I am especially grateful to my sister and brother-in-law Kate and Tim Slack for all their kindness and for allowing me to rummage among their books and periodicals; and to Rabbi Lionel Blue who has been constant in encouragement.

J.M.H.

The Venerable Bede
c. 673–735

The reader of Bede's works gains a very definite impression of his character. Bede reaches across the centuries to us as kindly, careful, shrewd and gentle – and somehow very English. He is regarded as the first great historian we have: his *History of the English Church and People*, completed in 731, is a precious source for late Roman and early Anglo-Saxon England. Bede spent most of his life as a Benedictine monk in the monastery of Jarrow in Northumbria, where the early Christian Saxon civilization showed its best side in learning, art and music, fertilized by both Roman and Celtic Christianity. Bede was a devout monk with a special love for the daily services of the monastery; it is recorded of him that he said:

I know that the angels are present at the Canonical Hours, and what if they do not find me among the brethren when they assemble? Will they not say, Where is Bede? Why does he not attend the appointed devotions with his brethren?

The following is Bede's description of the advice given to King Edwin by one of his nobles about accepting Christianity:

Another of the king's chief men . . . went on to say: 'Your Majesty, when we compare the present life of man with that time of which we have no knowledge, it seems to me like the swift flight of a lone sparrow through the banqueting hall where you sit in the winter months to dine with your thanes and counsellors. Inside there is a comforting fire to warm the room; outside, the wintry storms of snow and rain are raging. This sparrow flies swiftly in through one door of the hall, and out through another. While he is inside, he is safe from the winter storms; but after a few moments of comfort, he vanishes from sight into the darkness whence he came. Similarly, man appears on earth for a little while, but we know nothing of what went before this life, and what follows. Therefore, if this new teaching can reveal any more certain knowledge, it seems only right that we should follow it.'

From the account of Bede's last hours, given by his friend Cuthbert:

. . . at None he said to me, 'I have a few articles of value in my basket, such as pepper, linen and incense. Run quickly and fetch the priests of the monastery, so that I may distribute among them the gifts that God has given me.' In great distress I did as he bid me. And when they arrived, he spoke to each of them in turn, requesting and reminding them diligently to offer Masses and prayers for him. They readily promised to do so, and all were sad and wept, grieving above all else at his statement that they must not expect to see his face much longer in this world. But they were heartened when he said, 'If it be the will of my Maker, the time has come when I shall be freed from the body and return to Him who created me out of nothing when I had a long life, and the merciful Judge has ordered it graciously. The time of my departure is at hand, and my soul longs to see Christ my king in his beauty.' He also told us many other edifying things and passed his last day happily until evening. Then the same lad, named Wilbert (who had been helping Bede with his writings), said again: 'Dear master, there is one sentence still unfinished.' 'Very well,' he replied: 'write it down.' After a short while the lad said, 'Now it is finished.' 'You have spoken truly,' he replied: 'It is well finished. Now raise my head in your hands, for it would give me great joy to sit facing the holy place where I used to pray, so that I may sit and call on my Father.' And thus, on the floor of his cell, he chanted 'Glory be to the Father, and to the Son, and to the Holy Spirit' to its ending, and breathed his last.

Bede's concluding prayer at the end of the list of his writings:

I pray you, noble Jesu, that as you have graciously granted me joyfully to imbibe the words of Your knowledge, so You will also of Your bounty grant me to come at length to Yourself, the Fount of all wisdom, and to dwell in Your presence for ever.

—————————————— 2 ——————————————

Alfred the Great
849–901

In spite of inheriting a defeated and devastated kingdom in the early stages of the terrible Danish invasions, and the handicap of continual ill health for many years, this amazing man not only drove the Danes from Wessex, established forts, towns, churches and began the building of a fleet, reformed the law and struggled for justice, but found time to foster learning and all the arts of civilization , seeing them as part of the service of God. He was conscious of his inadequate education, but although not fully fluent in Latin, with the help of scholars he managed to translate and comment on books which he thought would be of use to his people: his explanations and amplifications are often of great interest as showing the Saxon mind at work. He is rightly remembered in his royal town of Winchester and also rightly (alone of English kings) given the surname 'the Great'.

From his work on St Augustine:

Therefore it is needful that thou look straight with the eyes of thy spirit to God, as straight as a cable stretches taut from a ship to her anchor. Then, as the anchor is fixed firmly in the earth, so do thou fasten thine eyes to God. Even though the ship tosses at sea in the waves, yet she is safe and unbroken as long as her cable holds fast to her anchor. And with these anchors – wisdom and humility and prudence and moderation and justice and mercy and reason and maturity of mind and goodwill and cleanness and abstinence – with these thou shalt fasten firmly to God the cable that shall keep safe the ship of thy soul.

--------------------------------- 3 ---------------------------------

St Dunstan
924–88

Out of over a hundred Archbishops of Canterbury, only five have met violent deaths, which compares well with the record of English kings. But almost every other tribulation has affected them – certainly St Dunstan had troubles enough. He apparently incurred unpopularity at court early in his career (accused of being a wizard, among other disagreeable slanders) but managed to restore his reputation and become Abbot of Glastonbury. He was skilled in the arts and exceedingly eager that the English church should be reformed and revived and especially that the monastic life should be re-established after the destruction of the Danish invasions. After he was made Archbishop of Canterbury in 960 he worked tirelessly to that end, having difficulties with various kings – it was only King Edgar with whom he was really able to co-operate. There is an account of the crowning of the king in 973 which shows how much the ceremony devised by Dunstan resembles that which still takes place today:

Two bishops led Edgar into the church while the choir sang an antiphon. The King prostrated himself before the altar, laid aside the crown (which he already wore) and Dunstan began the singing of the Te Deum, *but was so moved by the occasion that he wept for joy at the King's humility and wisdom. When the* Te Deum *was finished, the bishops raised the King and the archbishop administered to him the coronation oath. At this time the King swore: 'that the Church of God and all his Christian people shall keep true peace under our rule at all times; that I shall forbid thefts and every iniquity to every grade of man; that I shall ordain justice and mercy in all judgments, that the kindly and merciful God may grant to me and to you his mercy,' and to this all present said 'Amen'. After three prayers, came the solemn prayer calling down God's blessing 'on your servant Edgar, whom we have chosen with suppliant devotion for royal authority over Angles and Saxons,' and asking God to grant him the faithfulness of Abraham, the gentleness of Moses, the fortitude of Joshua, the humility of David, the wisdom of Solomon, and to help to nourish, instruct, fortify and build up the church of his kingdom and all the people committed to him, ending with the anointing by Dunstan in Christ's name and the antiphon 'Zadok the priest and Nathan the prophet' . . In the midst of further prayers, the King was given a ring and sword, symbols of royal power; then he was crowned, and sceptre and staff were placed in his hands; and a blessing pronounced over him. Then the King received the allegiance of his leading subjects, and was acclaimed: 'vivat rex, vivat rex, vivat rex in eternum . . .'*

William the Conqueror
?1028–87

Of all the Norman kings of England, none was so formidable as the great Conqueror himself. His whole life was a struggle: born the illegitimate son of Robert II, Duke of Normandy and Herleva (reputedly the daughter of a tanner at Falaise), he had to fight to keep his duchy from boyhood, then against France and Maine and finally to win and hold down England. It has been suggested that his marriage to Mathilda of Flanders was happy, but the softer side of this fierce Norman is not dwelt on by the chroniclers. As so often with mediaeval characters, the reader is frustrated by unanswered questions about them as people: the achievements are there, but not the spoken words. But at his deathbed the chronicles give what sound like actual spoken phrases:

The king passed the night of 8th September in tranquillity and awoke at dawn to the sound of the great bell of Rouen Cathedral. On his asking what it signified, his attendants replied: 'My lord, the bell is ringing for Prime in the church of Saint Mary.' Then the king raised his eyes and lifted his hands and said: 'I commend myself to Mary the holy Mother of God, my heavenly Lady, that by her intercession I may be reconciled to her Son our Lord Jesus Christ.' And having said this he died.

St Anselm
c. 1033–1109

St Anselm, consecrated Archbishop of Canterbury in 1093, was fundamentally a scholar and a theologian, who undertook heavy responsibilities when William Rufus and Henry I would have been difficult kings for any Archbishop to confront. He himself expressed his doubts as to the possibility of working with William Rufus, saying: 'You are yoking an untamed bull and a weak old sheep to the same plough.' The troubles which arose concerned where the boundary of power should be fixed between the King and the clergy – troubles that often arose in the Middle Ages. Anselm maintained his own views courageously, with the result that he was twice exiled (while in Rome he wrote a famous book on the Atonement), but in the end he was allowed to return to Canterbury. He carried on a long struggle to establish the authority of the See of Canterbury over that of York, believing that one authority was essential to the church in England, but the results were inconclusive. His *Prayers* and *Meditations* are thought to be the earliest of his writings that have survived.

Prayer to God:

> *Almighty God, merciful Father, and my good Lord,*
>   *have mercy on me, a sinner.*
> *Grant me forgiveness of my sins.*
> *Make me guard against and overcome*
>   *all snares, temptations, and harmful pleasures.*
>
> *May I shun utterly in word and deed,*
>   *whatever you forbid.*
>   *and do and keep whatever you command.*
> *Let me believe and hope, love and live,*
>   *according to your purpose and your will.*
>
> *Give me heart-piercing goodness and humility;*
>   *discerning abstinence and mortification of the flesh.*
> *Help me to love you and pray to you,*
>   *praise you and mediate upon you.*
> *May I act and think in all things according to your will,*
>   *purely, soberly, devoutly,*
>   *and with a true and effective mind.*
> *Let me know your commandments and love them,*
>   *carry them out readily, and bring them into effect.*
> *Always, Lord, let me go on with humility to better things*
>   *and never grow slack.*

Lord, do not give me over
  either to my human ignorance and weakness
  or to my own deserts,
  or to anything, other than your loving dealing with me.

Do you yourself in kindness dispose of me.
  my thoughts and actions, according to your good
  pleasure,
  so that your will may always be done
  by me and in me and concerning me.
Deliver me from all evil
  and lead me to eternal life
  through the Lord.

6

Anonymous
Mediaeval

Help us this day, O God, to serve Thee devoutly, and the world busily. May we do our work wisely, give succour secretly, go to meat appetitely, sit thereat discreetly, arise temperately, please our friend duly, go to bed merrily and sleep surely, for the joy of our Lord, Jesus Christ, Amen.

7

Henry II
1133–89

King Henry's life was one of incessant activity – his energy, like his boldness, seems to have been inexhaustible, as he coped with his vast possessions in England and France. His only real defeats were his failure to obtain and keep his family's loyalty and his inability to control the church through Thomas à

Becket, who had been his friend, but who, as Archbishop of Canterbury, was transformed into a defender of clerical privileges.

Henry is one of the earliest mediaeval characters for whom we have actual verbal pictures by the chroniclers – his appearance, stocky and unkempt; his habit of doodling and whispering during Mass; his indifference to discomfort and squalor while travelling, and, as in the passage below, what seems to have been actual echoes of his outspoken views.

When attempting a reconciliation with Becket:

'Have I not raised you from the poor and humble to the pinnacle of honour and rank? It hardly seemed enough for me unless I not only made you father of the kingdom but also put you even before myself. How can it be that so many favours, so many proofs of my affection for you, which everyone knows about, have so soon passed from your mind, that you are now not only ungrateful but oppose me at every turn?'

'Far be it from me, my lord,' said the archbishop, 'I am not unmindful of the favours which, not simply you, but God the bestower of all things has deigned to confer on me through you, so far be it from me to show myself ungrateful or to act against your wishes in anything, so long as it is agreeable to the will of God . . . You are indeed my liege lord, but He is lord of both of us, and to ignore His will in order to obey yours would benefit neither you nor me . . . Submission should be made to temporal lords, but not against God, for as St Peter says, "We ought to obey God rather than men."'

To this the king replied 'I don't want a sermon from you: are you not the son of one of my villeins?'

'It is true,' said the archbishop, 'that I am not of royal lineage: but then, neither was St Peter . . .'

─────────── 8 ───────────

The Black Prince
1330–76

Edward, Prince of Wales, the hero of Crécy and Poitiers and eldest son of King Edward III, died before his father, worn out by the hardships of campaigning in France and Spain. When he knew himself to be dying he made careful arrangements for his tomb in Canterbury Cathedral (where it can be seen to this day), took leave of his household and commended his little son, later Richard II, to his father and his brother John of Gaunt. Then:

. . . about 3 of the clock . . . he began vehemently to faint and so to lose his strength that scarce any breath remained in him, which the Bishop of Bangor, who was present, perceiving, he came unto him and said, 'Now, without doubt, death is at hand . . . therefore I counsel you, my lord, now to forgive all those that have offended you.' The prince managed to say 'I will,' but could not make any other intelligible sound, notwithstanding the pleas of the bishop who told him: 'It sufficeth not to say only "I will" . . . you ought to ask pardon.' The prince, despite his struggles, could not utter another word. The bishop realized that evil spirits were at work: taking the sprinkle he cast holy water by the four corners of the chamber where he lay, and behold, suddenly the Prince with joined hands and eyes lifted up to Heaven said: 'I give Thee thanks, O God, for all Thy benefits, and with all the pain of my soul I humbly beseech Thy mercy to give me remission of those sins which I have wickedly committed against Thee; and of all mortal men whom willingly or ignorantly I have offended, with all my heart I desire forgiveness.' When he had spoken these words he gave up the ghost.

Julian of Norwich
Fourteenth Century

The mediaeval church provided for an order of anchorites, who usually lived in a small room or house built on to the side of a church, with a window into the chancel so that they could participate in the Mass, and with another window or door into the outside world, so that visitors could come and talk to them and obtain counsel and comfort.

Julian of Norwich was such an anchorite, and she left a record of the sixteen 'showings' she received from Heaven. The message varies, but the underlying theme is the same: the overflowing love of God who wills that we love in return.

Again and again she emphasizes the love of God and his desire for our good – that prayer is, as it were, God in the soul lifting us up to God. Her book is one of the great classics of mediaeval spirituality

Prayer unites the soul to God, for though the soul may be always like God in nature and in substance restored by grace, it is often unlike him in condition through sin on man's part. Then prayer is a witness that the soul wills as God wills, and it eases the conscience and fits man to grace. And so he teaches us to pray and to have firm trust that we shall have it; for he beholds us in love, and wants to make us partners in his good will and work. And so he moves us to pray for what it pleases him to do.

10

Geoffrey Chaucer
?1340–1400

Geoffrey Chaucer was a royal servant for much of his life, starting as a page in the household of the Duke of Clarence, one of the sons of Edward III. He travelled abroad on royal business and read widely in French and Italian, which influenced his poetry. One of his most famous poems was in memory of Blanche, the beautiful first wife of John of Gaunt, Duke of Lancaster, another son of Edward III. Later, that same Duke was to marry Chaucer's sister-in-law, Katherine Swynford, so the Lancaster link became even closer: Gaunt and his son, Henry IV, were faithful patrons to Chaucer. When he died, in the first year of Henry's reign, he was buried in Westminster Abbey. His description of the country parson from the *Prologue* to the *Canterbury Tales* remained so true of many country priests over the centuries.

A holy-minded man of good renown
There was, and poor, the Parson to a town,
Yet he was rich in holy thought and work.
He also was a learned man, a clerk,
Who truly knew Christ's gospel and would preach it

Devoutly to parishioners, and teach it.
Benign and wonderfully diligent,
And patient when adversity was sent
(For so he proved in great adversity).
He much disliked extorting tithe or fee,
Nay rather he preferred beyond a doubt
Giving to poor parishioners round about
From his own goods and Easter offerings.
He found sufficiency in little things.
Wide was his parish, with houses far asunder,
Yet he neglected not in rain or thunder,
In sickness or in grief, to pay a call
On the remotest, whether great or small,
Upon his feet, and in his hand a stave.
This noble example to his sheep he gave,
First following the word before he taught it,
And it was from the gospel he had caught it.
This little proverb he would add thereto
That if gold rust, what then will iron do?
For if a priest be foul in whom we trust
No wonder that a common man should rust;
And shame it is to see – let priests take stock –
A shitten shepherd and a snowy flock
The true example that a priest should give
Is one of cleanness, how the sheep should live.
He did not set his benefice to hire
And leave his sheep encumbered in the mire
Or run to London to earn easy bread
By singing masses for the wealthy dead,
Or find some Brotherhood and get enrolled.
He stayed at home and watched over his fold
So that no wolf should make the sheep miscarry.
He was a shepherd and no mercenary.
Holy and virtuous he was, but then
Never contemptuous of sinful men,
Never disdainful, never too proud or fine,
But was discreet in teaching and benign.
His business was to show a fair behaviour
And draw men thus to Heaven and their Saviour,
Unless indeed a man were obstinate;
And such, whether of high or low estate,
He put to sharp rebuke to say the least.
I think there never was a better priest.

He sought no pomp or glory in his dealings.
No scrupulosity had spiced his feelings.
Christ and His Twelve Apostles and their lore
He taught, but followed it himself before.

Margery Kempe
Fifteenth Century

The Book of Margery Kempe gives an account of her prayers and visions whilst at home in Lynn in Norfolk, of her amazing travels and of her interviews with priests, monks, a bishop and even the formidable Archbishop Arundel, friend of Henry IV. It is a remarkable document: modern readers may often find themselves in sympathy with Margery's long-suffering husband and even with the people who reacted so violently against her weeping and exhortations. Some of the visions and temptations are hair-raising, but there is one description of a conversation with Christ which shows the gentleness which could overcome her:

Then answered Our Lord to her and said: 'I pray thee, daughter, give Me nothing but love. Thou mayest never please Me better than to have Me ever in thy love, nor shalt thou ever, in any penance that thou mayest do on earth, please Me so much as by loving Me. And, daughter, if thou wilt be high in Heaven with Me, keep Me always in thy mind as much as thou mayest, and forget Me not at thy meat, but think always that I sit in thy heart and know every thought that is there-in, both good and ill, and that I perceive the least thinking and twinkling of thine eye.'

Henry V
1387–1422

The impress of Shakespeare upon our imaginations concerning Henry V is so strong and so vivid, that trying to visualize the historic Henry is even more difficult than with most mediaeval kings. He seems, like so many of the members of the House of Lancaster, to have been exceedingly pious and careful to observe the ceremonies of the church of his time, eager to establish order and justice, but, in the manner of his age, either blind to or hardened to the appalling suffering that his righteous (as he considered) wars in France inflicted on so many innocent people.

His chaplain gave this description of his words on his deathbed:

It is certain that according to the will of our Saviour, to whom be praise, honour and thanks, I cannot avoid death which, according to the condition of all human flesh, is upon me. If, therefore, during my reign I have ruled otherwise than I ought, or done any injustice to anyone (which I do not believe), I ask his pardon. For the good services done me, particularly in this campaign, I thank you and your other fellow-soldiers; for which, if death had not cut short my intent, I proposed to reward each of you with fit recompense according to his deserts. I exhort you to continue in these wars till peace is gained; and I protest before God that I was not drawn into them by any ambitious desire for domination or vain-glory or worldly honour, or any other cause save only that by prosecuting my just title I might obtain both peace and my own rights; and I had been, before they began, most fully instructed by men of holy life, perfect and prudent, that I could and should enter upon them and bring them to a conclusion with this object in view, without danger to my soul . . .

The Paston Family
Fifteenth Century

The correspondence of this family of fifteenth-century Norfolk gentry survived, when so many similar family archives must have perished. It gives a fascinating view of their pre-occupations and crises: it was not just the warfare of the Wars of the Roses which impinged upon them, but the general state of disorder and easily aroused tumult endangered their houses and possessions – agitated descriptions pass between those at home in Norfolk and those endeavouring to exert influence whilst in attendance at Court. But the letters are not just filled with schemes to gain the help of some great man or of the king, Edward IV, himself: there are business dealings, a great amount of shopping to be done by the London end of the family and comment on the behaviour and matrimonial prospects of the younger generation.

Agnes Paston to her son John Paston (perhaps 29 October 1465) – it seems that there had been strained relations between them:

Son, I greet you well, and let you weet that, forasmuch as your brother Clement letteth me weet that ye desire faithfully my blessing, that blessing that I prayed your father to give you the last day that ever he spake, and the blessing of all saints under heaven, and mine, mote come to you all days and times. And think verily none other but that ye have it, and shall have it with that that I find you kind and willing to the weal of your father's soul, and to the welfare of your brethren.

By my counsel dispose yourself as much as ye may to have less to do in the world. Your father said, 'In little business lieth much rest.' This world is but a thoroughfare and full of woe, and when we depart therefro, right naught we bear with us but our good deeds and ill. And there knoweth no man how soon God will clepe him, and therefore it is good for every creature to be ready. Whom God visiteth, him he loveth.

And as for your brethren, they will I know certainly labouren all that in them lieth for you.

Our Lord have you in his blessed keeping, body and soul. Written at Norwich the 29th day of October by your mother, A.P.

Lady Margaret Beaufort
1443–1509

This forceful woman transmitted to her son, Henry VII, his claim to the throne as the surviving male heir of the House of Lancaster by the end of the Wars of the Roses. Three times married, she was notable in her last widowhood as an example of late mediaeval piety – of the effort to obtain salvation by works. As her confessor, Bishop John Fisher, described it, rising somewhat after five, after hearing the Mattins of Our Lady and the Mattins of the Day, she 'heard four or five masses upon her knees, so continuing in her prayers and devotions until the hour of dinner, which of the eating day was ten of the clock and upon the fasting day eleven. After dinner truly she would go to her stations to three Altars daily; her dirges and commendations she would say and her evensongs before supper.' When her rheumatism permitted it she would end the day with 'a large quarter of an hour' upon her knees in her chapel. She rigidly kept the feasts of the church and ate only one meal a day during Lent.

Tears, one of the most respectable contemporary marks of piety, Lady Margaret produced in copious measure – 'mervayllous wepyng' at her confessions and communions.

She was a generous patron of learning, instituting university readerships, and her benefactions to Cambridge re-founded the colleges St John's and Christ's. Bishop Fisher said of her after she died:

Who may not now take evident likelihood and conjecture upon this that the soul of this noble woman which so studiously in her life occupied in good works and with a fast faith of Christ and the Sacraments of his Church was defended in that hour of departing out of the body and was borne up into the country above with the blessed angels deputed and ordained to that holy mystery. For if the hearty prayers of many persons, if her own continual prayer in her lifetime, if the sacraments of the church, if indulgences and pardon granted by divers popes, if true repentance and tears, if faith and devotion in Christ Jesus, if charity to her neighbours, if pity upon the poor, if forgiveness of injuries, or if good works be available, as doubtless they be, great likelihood and almost certain conjecture we may take by them, and all these that so it is indeed.

15

Catherine of Aragon
1485–1536

Throughout the dangers and innovations of Henry VIII's break with Rome, his first queen maintained her integrity and her religion. All the children born to her had died, except Mary (later Queen Mary Tudor), and the king had persuaded himself that this was a sign from Heaven that he had been wrong to marry the widow of his elder brother Arthur – that the Papal dispensation was not valid for so serious a matter. Queen Catherine maintained steadfastly that she was indeed Henry's rightful wife and Queen. Sent away from court, with a sentence of annulment pronounced against her, knowing that Henry had married Anne Boleyn and was breaking England's ties with the Papacy, Catherine sent him a letter just before her death:

My most dear lord, king and husband: The hour of my death now drawing on, the tender love I owe you forceth me, my case being such, to commend myself to you, and to put you in remembrance with a few words of the health and safeguard of your soul which you ought to prefer before all worldly matters, and before the care and pampering of your body, for the which you have cast me into many calamities and yourself into many troubles. For my part, I pardon you everything, and I wish to devoutly pray God that He will pardon you also. For the rest, I commend unto you our daughter Mary, beseeching you to be a good father unto her, as I have heretofore desired. I entreat you also, on behalf of my maids, to give them marriage portions, which is not much, they being but three. For all my other servants, I solicit the wages due them, and a year more, lest they be unprovided for. Lastly, I make this vow, that mine eyes desire you above all things.

John Husee
?–1548

John Husee was the friend, helper and agent of Lord Lisle, Governor of Calais under Henry VIII, and his wife Honor. He acted as their go-between with the powerful courtiers in England and the king himself, keeping up a flow of presents of food and game, dogs and clothes and constantly watching out for his patrons' success. He seems to have been devoted to their interests and to have become a true friend. The following letter was written in 1537 when he heard that Lady Lisle was in distress as she had mistakenly thought herself pregnant:

. . . therefore good madam, in the honour of God, be not so faint hearted, ne mistrust not yourself. For I hope assuredly all is for the best; but I admit that it might chance otherwise (which God forbid), yet should not your ladyship take it so earnestly, but refer all unto God. For where his pleasure is, he will approve and feel faithful hearts, having full confidence in his mercy, which excelleth all worldly judgment. And yet, though your ladyship should chance to miss of your purpose, you should not be the first noble woman that hath been so by God's work visited. For if it be his pleasure he spareth neither Empress, Queen, Princess ne Duchess, but his handiwork must be suffered and his mercy abiden; and whatsoever is said or thought by any creature, God's work cannot be withstood.

Your ladyship can exhort and give others virtuous and good counsel, and now should it best appear in your own person, which both by your ladyship's writing and saying of others approveth for this time contrary. For I have heard of divers that your ladyship weepeth and sorroweth without comparison, which I assure your ladyship grieved me no less than it were my own mother. Therefore good madam, put your whole trust in God, and leave these sorrows, for he will never disdain you . . . I had liever die than your ladyship should despair in yourself . . .

17

Sir Thomas White
?1492–1567

Sir Thomas White of the Merchant Taylors' Company, the Muscovy Company, Sheriff and later Lord Mayor of London, was an example of the highly successful and charitable Tudor businessman. Amongst innumerable benefactions he was one of the founders of the Merchant Taylors' School and founder of St John's College, Oxford, to whom he addressed the following exhortation:

To Mr President, the Fellowes and Schollers of St Johns Colledge in Oxon.

I have mee recommended unto you even from the bottome of my hearte, desyringe the holye Ghoste may bee amonge you untill the end of the Worlde, and desyringe Almightie God that everye one of you may love one another as brethren; and I shall desyre you all to applye your learninge, and soe doinge GOD shall give you his blessinge both in this Worlde and in the Worlde to come. And furthermore if any variaunce or strife doe arise amonge you, I shall desyre you for Gods love to pacifye it as much as you maye; and that doinge I put noe doubt but GOD shall blesse everye one of you. And this shall be the last letter that ever I shall sende unto you, and therefore I shall desyre everye one of you to take a coppye of yt for my sake. Noe more to you at this tyme, but the Lorde have you in his keeping untill thende of the Worlde. Written the 27 of Januarye, 1566. I desyre you all to praye to God for mee that I maye end my life with patience, and that he may take me to his mercye.

By mee Sir Thomas White Knighte, Alderman of London, and Founder of St Johns Colledge in Oxforde.

Bishop Latimer
?1485–1555

Hugh Latimer was the son of a farmer and was sent to study at Cambridge, where he must have been affected by the group of Lutheran sympathizers known as 'Little Germany'. During the reign of Henry VIII he was frequently under suspicion for his reforming views, and in 1539 he resigned the Bishopric of Worcester because he could not support the anti-Protestant Act of Six Articles, passed in that year. In Edward VI's reign he came into his own and taught diligently – he was a renowned and greatly appreciated orator: one of his most famous sermons was 'Of the Plough' preached in the open air outside St Paul's Cathedral. He often preached before the king and did not mince words about the sins of courtiers.

In Queen Mary's reign he was martyred with Bishop Ridley at Oxford: it was he who said on the way to the stake, 'Be of good courage, Master Ridley, and play the man, for we shall today by God's grace light such a candle in England as shall never be put out.'

Shortly before that he had written to Ridley:

. . . there is no remedy (namely now when they have the master-bowl in their hand and rule the roast) but patience. Better it is to suffer what cruelly they will put upon us, than to incur God's high indignation. Wherefore, good my lord, be of good cheer in the Lord, with due consideration what he requireth of you, and what he doth promise you. Our common enemy shall do no more than God will permit him. God is faithful, which will not suffer us to be tempted above our strength. Be at a point what ye will stand unto; stick unto that and let them both say and do what they list. They can but kill the body, which otherwise is of itself mortal . . .

Archbishop Cranmer
1489–1556

The overwhelming personal magnetism of Henry VIII is shown in his dealings with Thomas Cranmer, whom he removed from academic life to be his Archbishop of Canterbury and his instrument against the Papacy. Henry must have terrified Cranmer – he terrified everyone – and certainly, from Cranmer's expressed views in later life, he must have had reservations about Henry's beliefs, as well as his behaviour; but in spite of everything, Henry seems to have inspired a genuine devotion in his Archbishop. And however much the king may have suspected that Cranmer's views were more reformist than his own, he steadfastly protected him from his enemies. After Henry's death Cranmer was able (in the Protestant atmosphere of Edward VI's reign) to produce his great First and Second Prayer Books for the Church of England, before his martyrdom under Queen Mary. But it was for Henry VIII that he wrote one of the most beautiful of all his compositions – Henry wanted a Litany in English, and Cranmer drew one up (substantially as we have it now) and it was published in 1545, so becoming the earliest portion of his work in the Book of Common Prayer. Unlike earlier Litanies (which were very repetitive) it combines variety with great ease for speaking even while going in procession in the open air, universality of application, marvellous cadences and one of the most moving sentences in the English language: 'In all time of our tribulation; in all time of our wealth; in the hour of death, and in the day of judgment, Good Lord, deliver us.'

A good example of Cranmer's sense of justice is his expostulation over Canterbury School when it was proposed to restrict it to gentlemen's sons:

> . . . but yet utterly to exclude the ploughman's son and the poor man's

son from the benefit of learning, as though they were unworthy to have the gifts of the Holy Ghost bestowed upon them as well as upon others, is as much as to say that Almighty God should not be at liberty to bestow his great gifts of grace upon any person, nor nowhere else but as we and other men shall appoint them to be employed according to our fancy and not according to his most godly will and pleasure; who giveth his gifts both of learning and other perfections in all sciences unto all kinds and states of people indifferently; even so doeth he many times withdraw from them and their posterity those beneficial gifts if they be not thankful. If we should shut up into a strait corner the bountiful grace of the Holy Ghost, and thereupon attempt to build our fancies, we should make as perfect a work thereof as those that took upon them to build the tower of Babylon; for God would so provide that the offspring of our best born children should peradventure become most unapt to learn and very dolts . . .

He had an answer for those who were always for severity in religion:

What will ye have a man do to him that is not yet come to the knowledge of the truth of the Gospel, nor peradventure as yet called, and whose vocation is to me uncertain? Shall we perhaps, in his journey coming towards us, by severity and cruel behaviour overthrow him, and as it were in his voyage stop him? I take not this way to allure men to embrace the doctrine of the Gospel.

At the time of his own martyrdom he fulfilled the prayer he had written as the Collect for the Fourth Sunday after Trinity:

O God, the protector of all that trust in thee, without whom nothing is strong, nothing is holy; Increase and multiply upon us thy mercy; that, thou being our ruler and guide, we may so pass through things temporal, that we finally lose not the things eternal: Grant this, O heavenly Father, for Jesus Christ's sake our Lord. Amen.

Thomas Becon

1512–67

In the upheavals of Mary Tudor's reign many Protestant clergy were forced to flee for their lives and Thomas Becon was one of them. He had been Chaplain to Protector Somerset in Edward VI's reign and later to Archbishop Cranmer. He was imprisoned in the Tower for a year at the beginning of Mary's reign, but being released from there managed to leave England and go to Strasbourg, which was a centre of English refugees. He wrote violently and savagely about the Catholics in his polemical works, and expostulated with Heaven about Mary's succeeding to the throne: 'Thou hast set to rule over us a woman, whom nature hath formed to be in subjection unto man, and whom thou by thine holy apostle commandest to keep silence . . . Ah, Lord! to take away the empire from a man, and give it unto a woman, seemeth to be an evident token of thine anger towards us Englishmen.' He returned to England in 1588 when Elizabeth became Queen (it is to be hoped that she never realized his attitude to women rulers) and was then restored to his rectorship of St Stephen Walbrook.

This prayer shows another side of his character:

O Heavenly Father . . . I most heartily thank Thee, that it hath pleased Thy fatherly goodness to take care of me this night past. I most entirely beseech Thee, O most merciful Father, to show the like kindness toward me this day, in preserving my body and my soul; that I may neither think, breathe, speak nor do anything that may be displeasing to Thy fatherly goodness, dangerous to myself, or hurtful to my neighbour; but that all my doings may be agreeable to Thy most blessed will, which is always good; that they may advance Thy glory, answer to my vocation, and profit my neighbour, whom I ought to love as myself; that, whensoever Thou callest me hence, I may be found the child not of darkness but of light; through Jesus Christ our Lord, Amen.

William Cecil, Lord Burghley
1520–98

The greatest of all the advisers to the Tudor monarchy was a character of much reserve, prudence and clarity of judgment and capable of maintaining his own opinions against Queen Elizabeth herself. His Protestant piety was undoubted: 'Serve God by serving of the Queen,' he once said, but it went much further than that. His own household was a model of good order and learning, where he was helped by his wife Mildred, herself learned and a patron of devout ministers. It was Burghley's custom to read through the Old Testament once a year, the New Testament four times a year, and to pray in Latin. An episode which shows his attitude to Holy Writ was when (late in the reign) the young Earl of Essex had been speaking 'nothing but war, slaughter and blood' at a Privy Council Meeting and Burghley, without saying anything, drew forth a book of psalms and pointed to the verse: 'Men of blood shall not live out half their days'. When Essex's headlong career ended on the scaffold, the old man's action took on the nature of a prophecy.

Burghley summed up his relationship with God and his Queen as follows:

> . . . *As long as I may be allowed to give advice, I will not change my opinion by affirming the contrary, for that were to offend God, to Whom I am sworn first, but as a servant I will obey Her Majesty's commandment, and no wise contrary the same, presuming that she being God's chief minister here, it shall be God's will to have her commandment obeyed, after that I have performed my duty as a counsellor and shall in my heart wish her commandments to have such good success as I am sure she intendeth.*

Bishop Jewel
1522–71

Controversy, in Tudor times between people of different faiths, was carried on in savage terms, and John Jewel could be as savage as many of his contemporaries. He escaped from England in Mary's reign to avoid arrest for Protestantism and returned under Elizabeth to be the first apologist for the Elizabethan Church of England. He was appointed Bishop of Salisbury in 1560 and built the Cathedral library there: he was also a noted patron of learned men.

This extract, from his *A Treatise of the Holy Scriptures*, shows the passionate devotion of the reformer to the Bible and a belief that the Holy Spirit will guide the earnest seeker:

But the Holy Spirit of God, like a good teacher, applieth himself to the dulness of our wites. He leadeth not us by unknown places of the earth, nor by the air, nor by the clouds: he astonieth not our spirits with natural vanities. He writeth his law in our hearts: he teacheth us to know him, and his Christ: he teacheth us that we should 'deny ungodliness and worldly lusts', and that 'we should live soberly, and righteously, and godly in this present world': he teacheth us to look for the 'blessed hope and appearing of the glory of the mighty God, and of our Saviour, Jesus Christ'.

Sir Henry Sidney
1529–86

Sir Henry Sidney was a friend and companion of the young King Edward VI and was with him when he died. He continued a faithful servant of the Tudor monarchy, holding, among other posts, that of Lord Deputy of Ireland and President of the Council for the Marches of Wales. He was married to Mary, sister of Robert Dudley, later the famous Earl of Leicester. The following is part of a letter of advice addressed to his son Philip in 1566 when the boy was eleven or twelve (the advice seems to have borne fruit).

Son Philip, I have received two letters from you, one written in Latin, the other in French: which I take in good part, and will you to exercise that practice of learning often; for that will stand you in most stead in that profession of life that you are born to live in. And now, since this is my first letter that ever I did write to you, I will not that it be all empty of some advice which my natural care of you provoketh me to wish you to follow, as documents to you in this your tender age.

Let your first action be the lifting up of your mind to Almighty God by hearty prayer; and feelingly digest the words you speak in prayer, with continual meditation and thinking of Him to whom you pray, and of the matter for which you pray. And use this as an ordinary act, and at an ordinary hour; whereby the time itself shall put you in remembrance to do that you are accustomed to do in that time.

Apply your study to such hours as your discreet master doth assign you earnestly . . . And mark the sense and the matter of that you do read as well as the words; so shall you both enrich your tongue with words and your wit with matter, and judgment will grow as years grow in you. Be humble and obedient to your masters, for, unless you frame yourself to obey others – yea, and feel in yourself what obedience is, you shall never be able to teach others to obey you. Be courteous of gesture and affable to all men, with diversity of reverence according to the dignity of the person; there is nothing that winneth so much at so little cost . . . Above all things tell no untruth; no, not in trifles. The custom of it is naughty . . . For there cannot be a greater reproach to a gentleman than to be accounted a liar. Study and endeavour yourself to be virtuously occupied. So shall you make such a habit of well doing in you as you shall not know how to do evil, though you would.

Edward VI

1537–53

Had he lived to manhood, the patron of Ridley, Latimer and Bucer might well have approved and encouraged a much more extreme Protestant system in England than actually developed under his sister Elizabeth. All accounts show his piety, his partisanship, his intelligence and his interest in the business of ruling. It does not appear that the King was in fact a very delicate or unhealthy boy until the last year of his life, when a complication of illnesses set in and caused him much lengthy suffering. In his last days his servants heard him murmuring a prayer, which he was too weak to write down, but which they recorded:

Lord God, deliver me out of this miserable and wretched life, and take me amongst thy chosen; howbeit, not my will but Thy will be done. Lord, I commit my spirit to Thee. O! Lord, thou knowest how happy it were for me to be with Thee: yet, for Thy chosen's sake, send me life and health, that I may truly serve Thee. O! my Lord God, defend this realm from papistry, and maintain Thy true religion, that I and my people may praise Thy holy name, for Thy son Jesus Christ's sake. Amen.

Queen Elizabeth I

1533–1603

It is ironical that the Church of England, which in its institutional aspect has no great love for clever women, should owe its existence and its form to the most brilliant woman of her generation. The research of the last fifty years has emphasized how it was the Queen's determination which preserved the Anglican *via media* between Geneva and Rome. Coming to the throne at the age of twenty-five, as the hope of the Protestants, after the Catholic persecutions of Mary's reign, she struggled successfully against her own devoted partisans to transmit a Catholic element in the Church. (There are comical moments in the struggle: some hot Gospellers saw fit to remove the silver cross from her own chapel while she was away one summer . . . the cross speedily returned.) Elizabeth Tudor has suffered more than most rulers from the limitations of historians, who have often been unable to realize that a caustic tongue concerning the clergy and a brisk financial attitude to them do not necessarily imply scepticism about religion itself. The Queen's own words unmistakably reveal the voice of faith: there is a mass of evidence to choose from, from the time when, accused of plotting against her sister, she was landed at Traitors' Gate of the Tower, in imminent danger of death as well as exposed to humiliating insult, and exclaimed: 'Here lands as true a subject as ever landed at these stairs. Before Thee, O God, do I speak it, having no other friend than Thee alone!'

The revealing words spoken to her various Parliaments have been recorded by Sir John Neale, as the following of 1586 when both Houses were pressing her to consent to the execution of Mary Queen of Scots and she was resisting them:

The bottomless graces and immeasureable benefits bestowed upon me by the Almighty are and have been such, as I must not only acknowledge them but admire them, accounting them as well miracles as benefits; not so much in respect of His Divine Majesty – with whom nothing is more common than to do things rare and singular – as in regard of our weakness, who cannot sufficiently set forth His wonderful works and graces, which to me have been so many, so diversely folded and embroidered one upon another, as in no sort am I able to express them. And although there liveth not any that may more justly acknowledge themselves infinitely bound unto God than I, whose life He hath miraculously preserved at sundry times (beyond my merit) from a multitude of perils and dangers, yet is not that the cause for which I count myself the deepliest bound to give Him my humblest thanks, or to yield Him greatest recognition; but this which I shall tell you hereafter, which will deserve the name of wonder, if rare things and seldom seen be worthy of account. Even this it is: that as I came to the crown with the willing hearts of subjects, so do I now, after twenty-eight years' reign perceive in you no diminution of good wills, which, if haply I should want, well might I breathe but never think I lived.

The most famous record of her religious belief, is, of course, the verse on the sacrament attributed to her by tradition:

> *Christ was the Word that spake it,*
> *He took the bread and brake it,*
> *And what that Word doth make it,*
> *That I believe, and take it.*

------------------------------ 26 ------------------------------

The Earl of Leicester
?1533–88

The exact date of Robert Dudley's birth is not known, but there was a tradition that he was born on the same day as Queen Elizabeth, 7 September 1533, and that this astrological matching accounted for the affinity between them. No one who saw them together doubted that affinity: from the time that he became Master of the Horse on her accession in 1558 until his death in Armada year he was her constant companion, and in some ways seems to have understood her better than any other human being was able to do. But he never succeeded in his aim of marrying her; he never achieved the final peak of Dudley ambition. He was the finest ornament of her court, but as she said herself: 'I will have here but one mistress and no master.' He was widely disliked for his pre-eminence, and in view of it, and of his pride, it is amazing that he should have responded as he did to a puritan (unknown to him) who wrote to rebuke him for his worldly way of life:

I will not justify myself from being a sinner of flesh and blood as others be. And besides, I stand on the top of a hill where I know the smallest slip seemeth a fall. But I will not excuse myself. I may fall many ways and have more witnesses thereof than many others who perhaps be no saints neither, yet their faults less noted, though some ways greater than mine . . . I never saw or knew in my life more envy stirring, and less charity used, every man glad to hear the worst, to think the worst, or to believe the worst of his neighbour, which be very uncomfortable fruits of our profession.

The Earl of Huntingdon
1536–95

It was dangerous in the sixteenth century to have any claim to the throne, however remote, and Henry Hastings, Earl of Huntingdon, suffered through being descended from Edward IV's brother as Queen Elizabeth felt that many of her subjects might think the Earl had a claim to succeed her. She was concerned, also, about his religious attitude: he was very devout, in the spirit of the Puritans, and was the first of the noble Elizabethans to maintain a 'godly household' and be a true supporter of preachers and reform. Huntingdon was married to Katherine, one of the sisters of Robert Dudley, Elizabeth's favourite, but his Protestantism seems to have been much more consistent than that of his famous brother-in-law. The Queen came to trust Huntingdon in the end, and made him Lord President of the Council of the North, a post of great importance as dealing with the whole of the Scottish border country.

When he died, his brother, a very puritan Anglican, wrote of him describing the type of nobility that the early reformers wished to see:

He was a sincere professor of God's truth and therein most zealous; a loyal servant to his sovereign, and for her service would spare neither purse nor pains; a careful man for his country being in public causes most provident, and in private most upright, loathing and detesting to seek gain by either; a most loving and tender hearted man to his kindred, for whom he held nothing that he had too dear; a most pitiful man to the poor, and devising continually how to do them good; a true friend to his friends, and ready always to perform the true part of an honourable friend to them, and an honest man to all men in all actions. Here have you a portrait of as perfect a man as flesh and blood can afford, and yet I do not avow him clean from all imperfections, but I dare avow him clean from any gross corruption or villainy . . .

---------- 28 ----------

Sir Francis Drake
?1540–96

We have a clearer image of Sir Francis Drake than of almost any other Elizabethan except the Queen herself; the engraving of him carries complete conviction: the short, stocky body, the round face, the broad competent hands, the great pear-drop pearl in the ear and the peascod doublet. He was the greatest of all the great seamen of the time – the first captain to circumnavigate the globe (Magellan, his predecessor, had died on the earlier voyage), the captain more than any other responsible for the defeat of the Armada, a man of extraordinary strategic and tactical powers. He was also a fervent Protestant and a devout Christian, and the following prayer is traditionally attributed to him:

O Lord God, when Thou givest to Thy servants to endeavour any great matter, grant us to know that it is not the beginning of the same, but the continuing of it until it be thoroughly finished, which yieldeth the true glory.

Before sailing to destroy the first Armada in Cadiz harbour, he wrote to his staunch supporter Sir Francis Walsingham:

The wind commands me away. Our ship is under sail. God grant we may so live in His fear as the enemy may have cause to say that God doth fight for Her Majesty as well abroad as at home . . . Pray unto God for us that He will direct us the right way; then we shall not doubt our enemies, for they are the sons of men.

Sir Walter Raleigh
?1552–1618

Of all the great Elizabethans few have provoked stronger reactions both for and against than Walter Raleigh. To his friends and admirers he was a man of original mind, a brave soldier and sailor against Spain, the founder of Virginia, a historian and a superb poet – what might now be called a 'life-enhancer'. To his enemies he was a vainglorious courtier, greedy for money and power and fame and heedless how he came by them. But when – after many and complex intrigues – he was not only confined in the Tower by James I but finally executed to placate the Spaniards whom James wished to conciliate, public opinion swung round in his favour and in admiration of his behaviour on the scaffold. He asked the people to pray for him, saying:

I have many sins for which to beseech God's pardon. Of a long time my course was a course of vanity. I have been a seafaring man, a soldier and a courtier, and in the temptations of the least of these there is enough to overthrow a good mind and a good man.

He finished by saying:

Give me heartily of your prayers, for I have a long journey to go.

It is said that the night before his execution he wrote in his Bible:

> *Even such is Time, that takes in trust*
> *Our youth, our joyes, our all we have,*
> *And pays us but with age and dust,*
> *Who in the dark and silent grave,*
> *When we have wandered all our ways,*
> *Shuts up the story of our days;*
> *But from this earth, this grave, this dust,*
> *My God shall raise me up, I trust!*

Sir Philip Sidney
1554–86

When Philip Sidney died of a wound received while
campaigning against Spain in the Netherlands, he had already
established an astonishing reputation for a man in his early
thirties as courtier, poet, translator and patron of the arts.
(Spenser dedicated *The Shepherd's Calendar* to him.) None of
Sidney's works were published in his lifetime, they were only
circulated in manuscript to his friends, but subsequently they
were of great importance in the history of English literature,
particularly, perhaps, *Astrophel and Stella*, the series of sonnets,
and his *Apologie for Poetrie*. He seems to have had an
indescribable gift of winning and keeping affection and was
deeply lamented by his fellow-writers.

The story is well known how, when he was being carried
wounded off the battlefield, they brought him some water, and
seeing a wounded soldier looking longingly at it he
immediately handed him the bottle, saying: 'Thy necessity is
yet greater than mine.'

The following is from *A Work concerning the Trewness of
Christian Religion*, which was translated from the French of a
Huguenot friend of Sidney's. Sidney was only able to complete
the preface and the first six chapters, but this is from his part:

*Let a man run from East to West, and from South to North; let him
ransack all ages one after another: and wheresoever he findeth any men,
there shall he find also a kind of religion and serving of God, with prayers
and sacrifices. The diversity whereof is very great, but yet they have always
consented all in this point, that there is a God. And as touching the
diversity which is in that behalf, it beareth witness that it is a doctrine not
delivered closely from people to people, but also bred and brought up with
every of them in their own climate, yea and even in their own selves.
Within these hundred years many nations have been discovered, and many
are daily discovered still, which were unknown in former ages. Among*

them some have been found to live without Law, without King, without house, going stark naked and wandering abroad in the fields, but yet none without some knowledge of God, none without some spice of Religion: to show unto us that it is not so natural a thing in man to love company, and to clad himself against hurts of the weather (which things we esteem to be very kindly) as it is natural unto him to know the author of his life, that is to say, God.

Bishop Andrewes
1555–1626

The Church of England acknowledges Bishop Lancelot Andrewes of Winchester as being one of its greatest teachers on prayer. The *Preces Privatae* were not printed in his lifetime; owing to the author's immense learning they were written in a mixture of English, Latin, Greek and Hebrew. (He took part in translating the Authorized Version of the Bible, published in 1611.) Bishop Andrewes gave an original copy of the Prayers to Archbishop Laud, which survives, as do some other manuscripts. The Prayers were published in their mixture of languages in the 1670s, but were translated into English in the nineteenth century (by Cardinal Newman, among others) and they then became widely loved by people of different denominations.

Bishop Andrewes seems to have been both humble, charitable and greatly concerned with education (particularly the University of Cambridge and Westminster School). He was greatly esteemed for his preaching by Queen Elizabeth and King James as they were both learned enough to understand his detailed examination of words in different tongues. He never married, and when he died he left his money in numerous thoughtful and charitable benefactions.

From *Points of Meditation Before Prayer*:

Thou art careful about many things: but one thing is needful.
But we will give ourselves continually to prayer and to the ministry of the word.

Watch ye and pray always, that ye may be accounted worthy to escape
  the things that shall come to pass.
Love the Lord all thy life and call upon Him for thy salvation.
Humble thy soul greatly: for the vengeance of the ungodly is fire and
worms.
A man can receive nothing except it be given.
If he prayed that was without sin, how much more ought a sinner to pray:
but God is a hearer, not of the voice, but of the heart.
More is done by groanings than by words: to this end Christ groaned, for
  to give us an ensample of groaning.
It is not that God desireth us to be suppliant or loveth that we lie prostrate:
                the profit thereof is ours and it hath regard to our advantage.
Prayer goeth up, pity cometh down.
God's grace is richer than prayer: God alway giveth more than He is asked.
God commandeth that thou ask, and teacheth what to ask, and promiseth
  what thou dost ask, and it
displeaseth Him if thou ask not: and dost thou not ask notwithstanding?
Prayer is a summary of faith, an interpreter of hope.
It is not by paces but by prayers that God is come at.
Faith poureth out prayer and is grounded in prayer.
Therefore go on to labour fervently in prayers
                        always to pray and not to faint
                        in spirit and in truth.
Faith is the foundation and basis of prayer: the foundation of faith is the
  promise of God.
Lift up your hearts.
He that made us to live, the same taught us withal to pray.
The prayer of the humble pierceth the clouds.
Prayer is colloquy with God.

32

John Donne
1573–1631

The famous Dean of St Paul's had a wild and exciting youth. He
had been on the expeditions against the Spaniards in Cadiz
and the Azores in the 1590s, then obtained a good position as
secretary to the Lord Keeper, but ruined his chances of

promotion by making a secret marriage with his employer's niece. He did not take holy orders until much later, and finally became Dean in 1621. His sermons were famous in his lifetime, much more famous than his poetry, and he often preached before Charles I. It is difficult to choose an extract, but the following was quoted by a Bishop who must himself have been a connoisseur of sermons:

> *He that cares not though the material church fall, I am afraid is falling from the spiritual . . . He that undervalues outward things in the service of God, though he begin at ceremonial and ritual things, will come quickly to call Sacraments but outward things, and Sermons and Public Prayers but outward things in contempt. Beloved, outward things apparel God, and since God was content to take a body, let us not leave Him naked and ragged.*

33

Archbishop Laud
1573–1645

William Laud's reputation (during his lifetime and since) has suffered because of his close involvement with matters of state. He was the chief ally of the formidable Earl of Strafford in implementing Charles I's aim of ruling without Parliament – what was known as the policy of 'thorough', though Charles, by their standards, was not thorough enough. Laud was also bitterly disliked by the Puritans for his opposition to their teaching and preaching, for his insistence on various ceremonies of which they disapproved and most of all for his concurrence in the brutal sentences passed by the Court of Star Chamber against dissidents. But as Archbishop his patronage of learning, his benefactions to Oxford and his love for St John's College there (where he built the exquisite 'Canterbury' quadrangle) show his generosity and his concern for education. His own neighbours in Lambeth must have loved him, as they thronged to comfort and bless him when he was taken to the Tower in 1641, to be imprisoned like Strafford, in consequence of the Long Parliament's enmity to them both. He was kept there throughout the First Civil War, but taken out and executed as an old man in 1645.

The following is his prayer for England:

'Lord, bless this kingdom, that religion and virtue may season all sorts of men: that there may be peace within our gates, and prosperity in all our borders. In time of trouble guide us, and in peace may we not forget Thee; and whether in plenty or in want, may all things be so ordered, that we may patiently and peaceably seek Thy Kingdom and its righteousness, the only full supply and sure foundation both of men and states; so that we may continue a place and people to do Thee service to the end of time.

34

Father Augustin Baker
1575–1641

David Baker was brought up as a Protestant, but was converted to Catholicism as a young man. Wishing to join the Benedictines, he travelled to Padua, but poor health forced him to come back to England, where he held various posts, finally being ordained a priest in France in 1619. In 1624 he was sent to be the Chaplain of a new community of Benedictine nuns in Cambrai, from where he moved to Douai and in 1638 was sent on a mission to England. At that time Roman Catholic priests could be executed as traitors if they were caught – he travelled about England secretly, ministering to his co-religionists until 1641; when, just as it seemed he would be captured, he fell very ill and died before the authorities could lay hands on him. He left behind him a large amount of writings on the spiritual life given the general title of *Holy Wisdom*.

He wrote of charitableness to our enemies:

The degrees of our love to (supposed) enemies are such as follows: 1. The first and lowest degree is not to revenge ourselves on them, nor to render evil for evil, by word or deed, in their presence or absence, privily or publicly, &c. (Indeed we ought to behave with much wariness towards those that in nature we find an averseness from, so as that if we cannot as yet conquer the resentments of nature, we were best to eschew meddling in matters that concern them.) 2. Not to be angry or offended at any ill offices that they may seem to have done us. 3. To forgive them whensoever they crave pardon. 4. To forgive them before they acknowledge their fault or seek to make amends. 5. Not to be contristated at their prosperity, nor deny any offices of charity to them, but to pray for them, to speak well of them, and to do kindness to them, to congratulate for any good success of theirs, and be cordially sorry for their misfortunes, &c. 6. To seek occasions of doing them some special good, yea, and for the procuring of such good, to undergo some discommodity, loss or prejudice. 7. To take part in their prosperities or adversities as if they were our own. 8. After the example of our Lord, to hazard, and even lay down our lives for their souls' good. 9. To conquer all resentment, even the inferior nature, and in simplicity of soul to judge all their ill offices to be affects of their charity, and not averseness. (Yet I doubt whether even in the most perfect the love to enemies can come to be transfused into inferior nature from the superior soul, as our love to God sometimes may be.) 10. To do all this purely for the love of God. These things we ought to do the best we can, and God will accept of our good-will, though our actions be not so perfect as we would wish they were.

35

The Earl of Strafford
1593–1641

Thomas Wentworth, a Yorkshireman, was one of the most able and forceful of the ministers of Charles I. As President of the Council of the North and then as Lord Deputy of Ireland he worked indefatigably to implement the policy of 'thorough' – to make Charles's personal rule without Parliament so efficient and successful that it would be accepted by the whole nation. His great ally was Archbishop Laud, but they were both defeated by a combination of circumstances, of which the implacable hostility of the puritan House of Commons to their policies and the vacillations and corruption of the court were the most fatal. When Strafford was put on trial for his life by Parliament the King promised him that he should not suffer.

But mob violence round the palace of Whitehall induced the King to give way to Parliament's wishes and to sign the Bill of Attainder for Strafford's execution. Charles never forgave himself for this weakness, and eight years later, before his own execution, he said that God had justly punished him for forsaking his best servant.

Strafford wrote a letter of farewell to his young son from the Tower:

My dearest Will, these are the last lines you are to receive from a father that tenderly loves you. I wish there were a greater leisure to impart my mind unto you, but our merciful God will supply all things by His grace, and guide and protect you in all your ways; to whose infinite goodness I bequeath you.

Be sure you give all respect to my wife [Will's stepmother], that hath ever had a great love unto you. Never be awanting in love and care to your sisters, but let them ever be most dear unto you: and the like regard must you have to your youngest sister; for indeed you owe it to her also, both for her father and mother's sake.

The King I trust will deal generously with you, restore you those honours and that fortune which a distempered time hath deprived you of together with the life of your father. Be sure to avoid as much as you can to inquire after those that have been sharp in their judgments towards me, and I charge you never to suffer thought of revenge to enter your heart.

And God Almighty of His infinite goodness bless you and your children's children; and His same goodness bless your sisters in like manner, perfect you in every good work, and give you right understanding in all things.

You must not fail to behave yourself towards my lady Clare your grandmother with all duty and observance; for most tenderly doth she love you and hath been passing kind unto me. God reward her charity for it. And once more do I, from my very soul, beseech our gracious God to bless and govern you in all, and join us again in communion with His blessed saints where is fullness of joy and bliss for evermore. Amen. Amen. Your loving father.

The Authorized Version of the Bible
1611

The Authorized Version of the Bible was presented to King James I with a dedication which is still printed in all copies. But there was also a lengthy introduction to the reader, which is not now always included, probably because of its very discourteous remarks to Puritans, Jews and Roman Catholics, combined with a slightly defensive note as if the translators and compilers were sensitive to the question as to why there should be yet another version when there were several available, especially the famous Geneva Bible, with its Calvinist marginal notes, dear to Puritans and used by such men as Cromwell and Bunyan. However, from about the time of the Restoration, the Authorized Version superseded the rest until the coming of modern translations in the 1880s.

At the end of *The Translators to the Reader* it melts into charity:

It remaineth that we commend Thee to God, and to the Spirit of his grace, which is able to build further than we can ask or think. He removeth the scales from our eyes, the vail from our hearts, yea, correcting our affections that we may love it above gold and silver, yea, that we may love it to the end . . . Others have laboured and you may enter into their labours. O receive not so great things in vain: O despise not so great salvation . . . It is a fearful thing to fall into the hands of the living God; but a blessed thing it is, and will bring us to everlasting blessedness in the end, when God speaketh unto us, to hearken; when he setteth his word before us, to read it; when he stretcheth out his hand and calleth, to answer, Here am I, here we are to do thy will, O God. The Lord work a care and conscience in us to know him and serve him, that we may be acknowledged of him at the appearing of our Lord JESUS CHRIST, to whom with the Holy Ghost be all praise and thanksgiving. Amen.

George Herbert
1593–1633

The amazing mixture in George Herbert of the exalted poet and the sensible country parson gives his work its unique flavour. He was a parish priest for three years only, in the living of Bemerton, near Salisbury, but his *A Priest to the Temple* is packed with holy and shrewd advice to the country parson, much of it still valid. (It is interesting that he emphasized that the parson's wife should be skilled in medicine and be able to help the parishioners in their sickness.)

This poem is included, because it says more about prayer in a compacter space than any other statement on the subject in English except the Lord's Prayer itself:

Prayer

Prayer the Churches banquet, Angels age,
*   Gods breath in man returning to his birth,*
*   The soul in paraphrase, heart in pilgrimage,*
The Christian plummet sounding heav'n and earth;
Engine against th' Almightie, sinners towre,
*   Reversed thunder, Christ-side-piercing spear,*
*   The six-daies world transposing in an houre,*
A kinde of tune, which all things heare and fear;
Softnesse, and peace, and joy, and love, and blisse,
*   Exalted Manna, gladnesse of the best,*
*   Heaven in ordinarie, man well drest,*
The milkie way, the bird of Paradise,
*   Church-bels beyond the starres heard, the souls bloud,*
*   The land of spices; something understood.*

Oliver Cromwell
1599–1658

Because of the great achievements of Oliver Cromwell, many of his sayings and his letters have been preserved, so we often see the Puritans and Independents of his army and his time through seeing him. The more we read about him the more we realize his awareness of the presence of God: his belief that God not only commanded and helped and strengthened, but showed his will through mighty works – 'Providences' – such as victory in battle. Cromwell's mind was incapable of seeing any separation between the secular and the sacred: every event of life was permeated by the action of God.

Cromwell's family and friends were very dear to him, and he suffered acutely from the death of his eldest son at seventeen (of which he said that St Paul's words 'I can do all things through Christ that strengtheneth me' saved his reason), his second son at twenty-one and his youngest daughter Bettie just before his own last illness. He was usually a compassionate man, but was occasionally liable to convulsions of impetuosity or fury, which accounted for some of his actions in Ireland, which have so sullied his memory.

In his dealings with his soldiers he showed his belief in religious liberty: they too, like Cromwell, believed God showed his will in 'Providences' and they followed their unbeaten General from Marston Moor to Worcester with their invincible battle-cry: 'The Lord of Hosts!' Independents of the independents, they told Parliament that they had not shed their blood to allow a fresh tyranny of presbytery to rule them in place of the tyrannies they had overthrown. Cromwell understood and shared their view and the last nine years of his life were a constant perplexity how to reconcile the need to govern England by the godly and the possibility of getting the godly to agree. He struggled on, dying at last on 3 September

1658, the anniversary of his 'crowning mercies' the victories of Dunbar and Worcester.

From a letter to his daughter Bridget Ireton, shortly after her marriage in 1645:

Your sister Claypole is, I trust in mercy, exercised with some perplexed thoughts. She sees her own vanity and carnal mind; bewailing it: she seeks after (as I hope also) what will satisfy. And thus to be a seeker is to be of the best sect next to a finder; and such an one shall every faithful humble seeker be at the end. Happy seeker, happy finder! Who ever trusted that the Lord is gracious, without some sense of self, vanity and badness? Who ever tasted that graciousness of His and could go less in desire – less than pressing after full enjoyment? Dear Heart, press on; let not Husband, let not anything cool thy affections after Christ. I hope he will be an occasion to inflame them. That which is best worthy of love in thy Husband is that of the image of Christ he bears. Look on that and love it best, and all the rest for that. I pray for thee and him; do so for me . . . I am thy dear Father, Oliver Cromwell.

When Charles I was imprisoned in the Isle of Wight in 1648, Cromwell wrote a long letter to the soldier, Colonel Robert Hammond, who was in charge of the King, which makes his views on 'Providences' very plain:

Thou desirest to hear of my experiences. I can tell thee: I am such a one as thou didst formerly know, having a body of sin and death; but I thank God, through Jesus Christ our Lord there is no condemnation, though much infirmity; and I wait for the redemption. And in this poor condition I obtain mercy, and sweet consolation through the Spirit. And find abundant cause every day to exalt the Lord, and abase flesh, and herein I have some exercise.

As to outward dispensations, if we may so call them: we have not been without our share of beholding some remarkable providences, and appearances of the Lord. His presence hath been among us, and by the light of His countenance we have prevailed. We are sure the goodwill of Him who dwelt in the Bush has shined upon us; and we can humbly say, we know in whom we have believed, who can and will perfect what remaineth, and us also in doing what is well-pleasing in His eyesight.

Jeremy Taylor
1613–67

Jeremy Taylor, who had been Chaplain to King Charles I and Archbishop Laud, suffered considerably in the Civil Wars and Interregnum, but was able to write a great deal, including his famous books *Holy Living* and *Holy Dying*. After the Restoration he was made Bishop of Down and Connor in Ireland. He was renowned as a preacher, one of his most famous sermons being a lengthy one on marriage, called: 'The Marriage Ring'.

From *Holy Living*, which is one of the shrewdest books on religion:

Remember that it is a great indecency to desire of God to hear those prayers a great part whereof we do not hear ourselves. If they be not worthy of our attention they are far more unworthy of God's.

And against the sin of curiosity:

Every man hath in his own life sins enough, in his own mind trouble enough, in his own fortune evils enough, and in performance of his offices failings more than enough, to entertain his own enquiry; so that curiosity after the sins of others cannot be without envy and an evil mind. What is it to me, if my neighbour's grandfather were a Syrian, or his grandmother illegitimate; or that another is indebted five thousand pounds, or whether his wife be expensive? But commonly curious persons (or, as the apostle's phrase is) 'busy-bodies' are not solicitous or inquisitive into the beauty and order of a well-governed family, or after the virtues of an excellent person; but if there be anything for which men keep locks and bars, and porters, things that blush to see the light, and either are shameful in manners or private in nature, these things are their care and their business.

Richard Baxter

1615–91

We have a picture of one of the great Puritans of the seventeenth century in Richard Baxter, a moderate man, whose long life was full of trials and cares. He was chaplain to Colonel Whalley's regiment in the Parliamentary army for some time after 1645, but became so ill that he had to leave it. He worked and wrote hard, though, in spite of illness, producing among other books the famous *Saints' Everlasting Rest* in 1650. At the Restoration of Charles II he did his best to effect a reconciliation between the Presbyterians and the Church of England, but was not successful and was much troubled by the triumphant Anglicanism of the time, being imprisoned by Judge Jeffreys in 1685–6, but the Toleration Act of 1689 rescued him from his greatest difficulties. One of his last actions was to write an appeal *The Poor Husbandman's Advocate* on behalf of country people who suffered desperately from poverty and the effect of poor harvests.

Baxter had long experience of preaching and teaching:

> *I heard of a preacher that would needs have his servant tell him what men said of his preaching; and being urged (but loth), he said: 'They say, sir, that you very often repeat the same things; and to tell you the truth, I think it is too true, for the last day you repeated that which you said divers days before.' Saith the master, 'Tell me what it was.' He paused awhile, and said, 'I remember not the words now.' Saith the master, 'Didst thou so understand them as to tell me the matter and meaning of them?' But he could tell neither. 'Nay, then,' saith the master, 'I will repeat them yet again for thy sake, and such as thou art.'*

Writing of the change of attitude that comes with age:

> *The Creed, the Lord's Prayer and the Ten Commandments do find me*

*now the most acceptable and plentiful matter for all my meditations. They
are to me as my daily bread and drink. And as I can speak and write of them
over and over again, so I had rather read or hear of them than of any of the
school niceties which once so much pleased me . . . I find in the daily
practice and experience of my soul that the knowledge of God and Christ,
and the Holy Spirit, and the truth of Scripture, and the life to come, and of
a holy life, is of more use to me than all the most curious speculations . . .
And as the love of God and the seeking of everlasting life is the matter of my
practice and my interest, so must it be of my meditation.*

From *Reliquiae Baxterianae*:

*I am deeplier afflicted for the disagreement of Christians than I was when
I was a younger Christian. Except the case of the infidel world, nothing is
so sad and grievous to my thought, as the case of the divided Churches.*

--------------- 41 ---------------

Colonel John Hutchinson
1616–64

The Republican party in the Civil War is vividly represented by
Colonel Hutchinson, whose life was chronicled by his wife in
her *Memoirs*, which remain one of the most lively accounts of
that time. He signed the death warrant of Charles I in 1649, for
which he was imprisoned after the Restoration and brought to
trial, but escaped the death penalty and was imprisoned
instead at Deal. Conditions there were so unhealthy that his
wife believed they brought on his illness and death. (He had
retired from public life in 1653, seven years before the
Restoration, probably from disapproval of Cromwell's
experiments with schemes of government which Colonel
Hutchinson thought betrayed the Republican cause.) Mrs
Hutchinson describes him minutely, not failing to mention his
neat and tidy way of dressing (sometimes very smartly, too,
which is an example of the resemblance between the Cavalier
and Puritan gentry, who were much closer in social habits than
is often suggested). Their marriage was a love match, and Mrs
Hutchinson describes his attitude to her:

45

So constant was he in his love, that when she ceased to be young and lovely, he began to show most fondness; he loved her at such a kind and generous rate as words cannot express; yet even this, which was the highest love he or any man could have, was yet bounded by a superior, he loved her in the Lord as his fellow-creature, not his idol, but in such a manner as showed that an affection, bounded in the just rules of duty, far exceeds every way all the irregular passions in the world. He loved God above her, and all the other dear pledges of his heart, and at his command and for his glory cheerfully resigned them.

42

The Agreement of the People
1649

January 1649 was the time of crisis in England when King Charles I was tried and executed. But, simultaneously, representatives of the more radical elements in Cromwell's army produced a new version of their *Agreement of the People*, over which they had laboured in 1647 and which they subsequently expanded. The passage on religion gave the view of many of the rank and file of the soldiers – hopes which were to go unfulfilled for over two centuries, but which not all the reactionary power of church and state could smother for ever:

Concerning religion, we agree as followeth:—
1. It is intended that the Christian Religion be held forth and recommended as the public profession in this nation, which we desire may, by the grace of God, be reformed to the greatest purity in doctrine, worship and discipline, according to the word of God; the instructing the people thereunto in a public way, so it be not compulsive; as also the maintaining of able teachers for that end, and for the confutation and discovering of heresy, error and whatsoever is contrary to sound doctrine, is allowed to be provided for by our Representatives; the maintenance of which teachers may be out of a public treasury, and, we desire, not by tithes: provided that Popery or Prelacy be not held forth as the public way or profession in this nation. 2. That, to the public profession so held forth, none be compelled by penalties or otherwise; but only may be endeavoured to be won by sound doctrine and the example of a good conversation. 3. That such as profess

faith in God by Jesus Christ, however differing in judgment from the
doctrine, worship or discipline publicly held forth, as aforesaid, shall not be
restrained from, but shall be protected in, the profession of their faith and
exercise of religion, according to their consciences, in any place except such
as shall be set apart for the public worship; where we provide not for them,
unless they have leave, so as they abuse not this liberty to the civil injury of
others, or to actual disturbance of the public peace on their parts.

43

John Evelyn
1620–1706

Of all Stuart country gentlemen of whom we have knowledge,
John Evelyn had the widest interests including public affairs,
travel, the arts, polite learning, gardening, court gossip, the
need to plant trees, new discoveries and his own soul. He
could be censorious, he could be over-convinced of the
nobleness of his own motives, however mixed they may seem
to us, but the prayer he wrote on his eightieth birthday is
moving in its simplicity and shows the genuine devoutness
which was so much a part of him:

I with my soul render thanks to God, who, of His infinite mercy, not
only brought me out of many troubles, but this year restored me to health,
after an ague and other infirmities of so great an age, my sight, hearing,
and other faculties tolerable, which I implore Him to continue, with the
pardon of my sins past, and grace to acknowledge by my improvement of
His goodness the ensuing year, if it be His pleasure to protract my life, that
I may be the better prepared for my last day, through the infinite merits of
my blessed Saviour, the Lord Jesus, Amen.

George Fox
1624–91

The founder of the Society of Friends (Quakers) was notable not only for his testimonies, his journeyings, his courage under persecution and imprisonment, but for his shrewd and lively letters to all Friends in time of need. The courage of the early Friends is one of the most glorious witnesses to integrity in English history. They were constantly abused and persecuted for their refusal to take oaths, to go to church, to accommodate themselves to the religious conventions of their time, to bear arms, to show special reverence to those in authority, but they remained true to their 'Inner Light'.

To Friends in New Jersey and Pennsylvania

Dear Friends,

With my love to you all, in God's holy peaceable Truth, and my desires are that you may all be kept careful of God's glory. Now in your settling of plantations and provinces, and especially in woody countries, you may have many trials and troubles, but if you keep in the wisdom of God, that will keep you both gentle, and kind, and easy to be entreated one of another, and that will preserve you out of heats, or extremes, or passions.

And I desire that you may be very kind and courteous to all in necessity, in the love of God; for there are many people goes over to your countries, some poor and some rich; and so, many eyes are upon you. And therefore my desire is that you may all be careful in the love of God, and in his truth and righteousness, as the family of God, and be careful and tender to all your servants in all respects.

And dear Friends, I desire that you would send over an account by the next ship how many Meetings you have, and let us know how Truth spreads and prospers amongst you; which you would do well to write every year, to the Yearly Meeting at London.

G.F. *1682*

To Friends that are prisoners at York

Dear Friends,

With my love to you all, and all the rest of the faithful Friends in bonds; and my desire is to the Lord that ye all may stand faithful and valiant for his glorious name, and his holy peaceable Truth now in this day of storm and tempest, that none may turn their backs on the Lord in this day of trial, and none be ashamed of confessing of Christ.

Mind the Lord in all your sufferings, and keep all low, and in the humility of heart, and there you will feel that he that inhabits eternity dwells with an humble heart; and he will be your shield and buckler, and defender in time of trouble; and therefore do not think time long, and your sufferings long, for the Lord will lay no more upon you, but what you are able to bear. I know it, and am a witness for God in all my sufferings and imprisonments, and halings before magistrates about sixty times, about this thirty-six year. And so, Friends, when you are tried, you may come forth more precious than gold that is tried in the fire.

And though you be in outward bonds from your wives, families, houses and relations, yet the word of God is not bound: It's at liberty; it abides and endures for ever. It will make you all rich, though they think to make you poor with their bonds, and cast you into prisons, but I tell you, the word of God will make you rich, for the word of God was before the wicked and his bonds were; for in the beginning was the word, but since the beginning was the Devil.

In Christ you have heavenly peace: that none can take away from you. In him live and dwell.

G.F. 1682

Dear Friends,

Something was upon me to write unto you, that such among Friends, who marry and provide great dinners, that instead thereof, it will be of a good savour on such occasions, that they may be put in mind at such times to give something to the poor that be widows and fatherless, and such like, to make them a feast, or to refresh them. And this I look upon would be a very good savour, to feast the poor that cannot feast you again, and would be a good practice and example. And I do really believe, that whatever they give, less or more, according to their ability, cheerfully, they will not have the less at the year's end, for the Lord loves a cheerful giver.

I know this practice hath been used by some twenty years ago. And so it is not only to give the poor a little victuals, which you cannot eat yourselves, but give them a little money, that the Lord hath blessed you withal; and give it to some of the Women's Meetings for to distribute to the poor. These things I do recommend to you (though it may look a little strange) to weigh and consider the thing. It will be both of a good report,

49

and a good savour, and manifests a self-denial and openness of heart, and of the general love of God.

G.F.

London, the 4th of the 4th Month, 1690.

45

Dorothy Temple
1627–95

One of the most grievous parts of seventeenth-century books of devotion is where they try to explain and inculcate resignation to God concerning the deaths of children. Writings which reveal spiritual power and comfort fail here – the high death rate of children at that time made it a common sorrow, but it was as devastating then as now, beyond the reach of explanation. Devout Christians tried to accept it as the will of God, but the pain remained.

Dorothy Osborne, who happily married the famous diplomatist Sir William Temple after a long courtship, recorded in her famous *Letters*, had many children. But they all died in infancy or childhood, except one son and daughter, and the son, as a young man, committed suicide by drowning, apparently in a moment of acute depression. Lady Temple wrote to her nephew:

Dear Nephew – I give you many thanks for your kind letter and the sense you have of my affliction, which truly is very great. But since it is laid upon me by the Hand of an Almighty and Gracious God, that always proportions His punishments to the support He gives with them, I may hope to bear it as a Christian ought to do, and more especially as one that is conscious to herself of having many ways deserved it. The strange revolutions we have seen might well have taught me what this world is, yet it seems it was necessary that I should have a near example of the uncertainty of all human blessings, that so having no tie to the world, I may the better prepare myself to leave it; and that this correction may suffice to teach me my duty must be the prayer of your affectionate aunt and humble servant, D. Temple.

John Bunyan
1628–88

The son of a tinker of Harrowden, near Bedford, John Bunyan was conscripted into the army in the Civil War and served for three years before taking up his father's trade. After a long period of spiritual perplexity and suffering he gained the assurance of God's love to him, and from the 1650s onwards preached, wrote and taught with great effect. He was an Independent, a Baptist (but not, apparently, a 'strict' Baptist). After the Restoration in 1660, he suffered severely for his beliefs, being imprisoned for twelve years. His young and devoted wife did everything she could to obtain his release, even travelling to London to plead with the judges, but without effect. Bunyan worked in prison at making 'tagg'd laces' but the family must have been very poor. He said of himself: 'O, I saw in this condition I was as a man who was pulling down his house upon the head of his Wife and Children; yet thought I, I must do it, I must do it.' He wrote a great deal – in 1666 his spiritual autobiography: *Grace Abounding to the Chief of Sinners*, before his final release in 1677. In 1678 the first part of *The Pilgrim's Progress* was published (the second was issued in 1684). It was an immediate and widespread success. The theme, the journey of the soul to heaven, is of eternal significance; but the way the story is told, the mixture of folklore, the life of Bedfordshire in the 1670s and the life of the Bible, has an amazing impact on the reader building up to the overwhelming climax of the pilgrims, often so justly alarmed at the perils of the journey, descending into the River of Death with great courage and comfort – most of all the heroic Mr Valiant-for-Truth, about whom Bunyan wrote:

Then he said, 'I am going to my Father's, and tho with great Difficulty I am got hither, yet now I do not repent me of all the Trouble I have been at to arrive where I am. My Sword, I give to him that shall succeed me in my Pilgrimage, and my Courage and Skill, to him that can get it. My Marks and Scarrs I carry with me, to be a witness for me, that I have fought his Battels, who now will be my Rewarder.' When the Day that he must go hence was come, many accompanied him to the River side, into which, as he went, he said, 'Death, where is thy Sting?' And as he went down deeper, he said, 'Grave, where is thy Victory?' So he passed over, and the Trumpets sounded for him on the other side.

47

Charles II
1630–85

The changes of policy, the deviousness and the discretion of Charles II prevented his contemporaries from knowing his true religious feelings during his lifetime. The impression received is that his conversion to Catholicism – in the sense of mental assent to its truth – took place secretly, perhaps about 1670, under the influence of his sister Minette, herself a devout Catholic. But it was not acknowledged until his death, and even then the last rites had to be administered privately, to protect those involved. It was Father Huddleston, who had helped Charles escape after the battle of Worcester many years before and who was sheltered in the palace in 1685 to protect him from anti-Catholic feeling, who received Charles into the Church. When he brought the sacrament, Charles, who was desperately ill and in great pain, struggled to rise, saying: 'At least let me meet my heavenly Lord in a better posture than in my bed.' Father Huddleston calmed him: Almighty God, who saw into his heart, would accept his good intention. So the King received the Catholic communion and afterwards Huddleston sat quietly by him, reading the Catholic prayers for the dying in a low voice. It was by Charles' own request that Huddleston recited once again the Act of Contrition, ending 'Mercy, Sweet Jesus, Mercy'. Then the priest put a crucifix into the King's hands, saying that it only remained to him to meditate on the death and passion of 'Our dear Saviour Jesus Christ'.

Father Huddleston recited more prayers as the King held the crucifix: 'Beseech Him with all humility, that His most precious Blood may not be shed in vain for you . . . and when it shall please Him to take you out of this transitory world, to grant you a joyful resurrection, and an eternal crown of glory in the next.'

48

Archbishop Tillotson
1630–94

John Tillotson, who was promoted directly from the Deanery of St Paul's to be Archbishop of Canterbury in 1691, seems to have been a reconciler all his life. He had been brought up in the Free Church tradition, and was married to a niece of Oliver Cromwell, but conformed to the Church of England in Charles II's reign and used all his strength, then and later, to promote toleration. He was admired as a preacher and believed in the usefulness of preaching: 'Good preaching and good living', he said, 'will gain upon people.'

Tillotson had been instrumental in converting the Earl of Shrewsbury (known as the 'King of Hearts' because of his engaging manners and handsome face), to Anglicanism from Roman Catholicism in 1679, but he seems to have heard unsatisfactory reports of the Earl's conduct, because a few months later he wrote:

It was a great satisfaction to me to be anyways instrumental in the gaining of your Lordship to our religion, which I am most firmly persuaded to be the truth; but yet I am, and always was more concerned that your Lordship should continue a virtuous and good man than become a Protestant, being assured that the ignorance and errors of man's understanding will find a much easier forgiveness with God than the faults of their wills.

I remember your Lordship once told me that you would endeavour to justify the sincerity of your change by a conscientious regard to all the other parts and actions of your life: I am sure you cannot more effectually condemn your own act than by being a worse man after your profession.

The Archbishop made a very strong attack on the extremes to which the Calvinist doctrine of Predestination had been carried, when it was stated that God had decided before the foundations of the world who should be saved and who should be lost.

I am as certain that this doctrine cannot be of God as I am that God is good and just, because this grates upon the notion that mankind have of goodness and justice. This is that which no good man would do, and therefore it cannot be believed of infinite goodness. If an Apostle, or an angel from Heaven teach any doctrine which plainly overthrows the goodness and justice of God, let him be accursed. For every man hath greater assurance that God is good and just than he can have of any subtle speculations about predestination and the decrees of God.

———————————————— 49 ————————————————

Samuel Pepys
1633–1703

The famous Diary of Samuel Pepys gives a most vivid picture of London in the mid-seventeenth century. But it is the diary of a young man and being written with amazing honesty and lack of hypocrisy gives, in some ways, a one-sided picture of Pepys. For example, in those pages the great and famous naval administrator is only beginning his career. The later Pepys, with his friendships with so many learned men, his wide correspondence, his philosophic and scientific curiosity, is a character who has developed from the vital, impulsive, but always inquisitive writer of the 1660s. The Diary gives the impression of a man born in a Puritan environment, but who has moved out of it and now takes religion matter-of-factly, a severe critic of the clergy and their services, someone still given to making vows to God, but not always matching professions with action.

The account of his last days shows the other side – how reflection and consideration had deepened his faith. His friend Hickes, who attended him then and conducted the funeral, gave his witness:

The greatness of his behaviour, in his long and sharp tryall before his death, was in every respect answerable to his great life; and I believe no man ever went out of this world with greater contempt of it, or a more lively faith in every thing that was revealed of the world to come. I administered the Holy Sacrament twice in his illness to him . . . Twice I gave him the absolution of the Church, which he desired, and received with all reverence and comfort; and I never attended any sick or dying person that dyed with so much Christian greatness of mind, or a more lively sense of immortality, or so much fortitude and patience, in so long and sharp a tryall, or greater resignation to the will, which he most devoutly acknowledged to be the wisdom of God; and I doubt not but he is now a very blessed spirit . . .

50

The Marquess of Halifax
1633–95

It is not easy to be a moderate in an immoderate age, and Halifax, known as the 'Trimmer', was abused by both Whigs and Tories; he defended the right of the Duke of York, later James II, to succeed his brother Charles II at a time when extremists would have excluded the Duke because of his faithful Catholicism. Later, when James II had failed as a king Halifax was one of William and Mary's supporters, though far from being a blind partisan of the new monarchy. He received small thanks for his moderation and seems to have felt it deeply. During all the political storms of the time he wrote on political and semi-political matters, though it was not always expedient to publish his productions. One of his most famous works was his *Advice to a Daughter*, from which the following extract is taken:

The first thing to be considered is Religion. It must be the chief object of your thoughts, since it would be a vain thing to direct your behaviour in the world and forget that which you are to have towards him who made it. In a strict sense, it is the only thing necessary; you must take it into your mind and from thence throw it into your heart, where you are to embrace it so close as never to lose the possession of it.

But then it is necessary to distinguish between the reality and the pretence . . . The next thing to be observed to you is that religion doth as little consist in loud answers and devout convulsions at church, or praying in an extraordinary manner. Some ladies are so extreme stirring at church that one would swear the worm in their conscience made them so unquiet . . . Let your earnestness therefore be reserved for your closet, where you may have God Almighty to yourself; in public be still and calm, neither indecently careless, nor affected in the other extreme.

It is not true devotion to put on an angry zeal against those who may be of a differing persuasion. Partiality to ourselves makes us often mistake it for a duty to fall hard upon others in that case; and being pushed on by self conceit, we strike without mercy, believing that the wounds we give are meritorious, and that we are fighting God Almighty's quarrel, when the truth is we are only setting out ourselves . . . Nothing is so kind and inviting as true and unsophisticated religion: instead of imposing unnecessary burdens upon our nature, it easeth us of the greater weight of our passions and mistakes; instead of subduing us with rigour it redeemeth us from the slavery we are in to ourselves, who are the most severe masters whilst we are under the usurpation of our appetites let loose and not restrained.

Religion is a cheerful thing, so far from being always at cuffs with good humour that it is inseparably united to it . . . Religion is exalted reason, refined and sifted from the grosser parts of it; it dwelleth in the upper region of the mind, where there are fewest clouds or mists to darken or offend it; it is both the foundation and the crown of all virtues; it is morality improved and raised to its height by being carried nearer heaven, the only place where perfection resideth; it cleanseth the understanding and brusheth off the earth that hangeth about our souls.

51

The Earl of Rochester
1647–80

Henry Wilmot, later Earl of Rochester, shared Charles II's dangers in his escape from England after the Battle of Worcester. He died in 1658, leaving an eleven-year-old son, John, who grew up to be a poet, a wit and one of the wildest young men of the Restoration court, naturally looked on with kindness by Charles on account of his father's services. His

cruel satires and lampoons on Charles and his dangerous
escapades caused him to be sent away from court from time to
time, but he managed to return to favour. The spoilt young
courtiers were a callous society: the King's great minister,
Clarendon, wrote of them '. . . the very mention of good
nature was laughed at, and looked upon as the mark and
character of a fool; and a roughness of manners or hard-
heartedness and cruelty was affected.' Rochester seems to
have been bitterly aware of this, even while involved in it,
composing his icy *Satyr against Mankind* by 1676. None of this
stifled his interest in philosophy or in the nature of man and
from October 1679 he was talking of religion to Gilbert Burnet,
the famous preacher and author of the *History of the Reformation*. Their conversations, and Rochester's doubts, were recorded by Burnet himself. In May 1680 Rochester fell very ill in
Somerset and was visited by his mother's chaplain, who found
him suffering from doubts and fears as well as physical pain.
The chaplain, Robert Parsons, did everything possible for him
and one day read him the fifty-third chapter of Isaiah,
concerning the 'suffering servant'. Burnet described what
happened, as Rochester had told him.

*. . . as he heard it read, he felt an inward force upon him, which did so
enlighten his Mind, and convince him, that he could resist it no longer: For
the words had an authority which did shoot like Rays or Beams in his
Mind; so he was not only satisfied in his Understanding, but by a power
which did so effectually constrain him, that he did ever after firmly believe
in his Saviour, as if he had seen him in the clouds.*

Rochester called in all his servants, even the 'piggard boy'
who kept the pigs, and read them all a declaration of
repentance for his past life. Burnet arrived later and assured
him that there was hope for a sinner even on his deathbed if his
mind was 'truly renewed and turned to God'. Rochester
assured him that 'his mind was entirely turned; and though
Horrour had given him his first Awaking, yet that was now
grown up into a settled Faith and Conversion'. He died
peacefully a short while later.

William III
1650–1702

It is not always easy to acknowledge obligations and the English have been slow to appreciate the magnitude of what William III achieved for this country and for Europe. (It is sad, too, that this most tolerant of men has been invoked for intolerance in Ireland.) When in 1688 William answered the invitation of the 'Immortal Seven' – the statesmen who felt that only he could cope with the misgovernment of James II – he probably did not foresee the immediate kingship which was to follow. Having it, he found himself in exile from his beloved Netherlands and surrounded by an English aristocracy which had been corrupted during the reigns of Charles II and James II until many of them had become untrustworthy, idle, useless for war, government or foreign affairs and (so the Dutch ladies remarked) dirty. Many of the English found William reserved, abrupt and sardonic. The common soldiers, who saw him in battle, felt differently. Traditionally their comment was: 'Brave! Brave! By Heaven, he *deserves* a crown!' His Calvinism permeated his whole life and he was supported by a complete surrender to the will and purposes of God. Bullets through his sleeve, his hair or his coat were disregarded – he knew God's protection would cover him as long as God wished for his services.

His comment on a terrifying attack of smallpox as a young man was:

It has pleased the good God to restore me to perfect health . . . What distressed me most during my illness was having to spend three weeks without doing anything whatever. You can imagine how much was neglected during that time – but it was the will of heaven and one must be patient.

When he was still in his twenties, but already embroiled in

his struggles against Louis XIV and France, he said he had seen:

> . . . *a poor old man, tugging alone in a little boat with his oars, against the eddy of a sluice, upon a canal; that, when with the last endeavours he was just got up to the place intended, the force of the eddy carried him quite back again; but he turned his boat as soon as he could, and fell to his oars again; and thus three or four times while the Prince saw him; and concluded, this old man's business and his were too like one another, and that he ought, however, to do just as the old man did, without knowing what would succeed, any more than what did in the poor man's case.*

A month after his wife died he wrote to a friend in Holland:

> *The irreparable loss with which it has pleased the good God to chastise me has rendered me incapable of writing to you . . . I shall all the same endeavour as much as in me lies to do my duty, hoping that the good God will give me strength for it.*

53

Mrs Burnet
1661–1709

Mrs Burnet, the wife of Gilbert, Bishop of Salisbury and historian of the Reformation, wrote a book, *A Method of Devotion*, for members of the Church of England, providing prayers and meditations for all sorts of people and occasions, even for handsome girls and plain girls. In the account of her life, given as an introduction to the book after her death, it was explained that she had come to think very seriously about her faith because she had been married as a young woman to a Roman Catholic, and therefore necessarily thought seriously about Anglican beliefs when her new family explained their own views. But the book is free from controversy, and is concerned with the inner life of spirituality and its impact on behaviour. In her own case, her piety resulted in a great and wise charitableness, in which her second husband, the Bishop, warmly supported her.

From *A Prayer Before Reading the Holy Scriptures*:

O Infinite Wisdom! tho' I am not worthy to open this Book, and unable to loose the Seals, to comprehend the Depths thereof; yet I humbly beg, for the sake of Christ Jesus, the Lamb of God, and who has by his precious Blood obtained for us Redemption from Sin, and Reconciliation with God, and has promised his Holy Spirit to those that ask it: For his Sake and in virtue of that Promise, I beg such a Degree of Spiritual Light, as may produce in me saving Faith and entire Obedience; that so what was ordained unto Life, may not be, through my Fault, the Cause of Death. O Lord, I am persuaded, that all things needful to be known or done, in order to my being happy here, and hereafter, are contained in thy holy Word.

O let not Pride, Self-Conceit, or any other Vice, lead me into Error: Pardon my Weakness and unwilling Mistakes; and grant I may grow in the knowledge and Love of Thee, my God, and thy Son Jesus Christ, my Lord; to whom with Thee and the Holy Spirit be Glory for ever.

————————————————— 54 —————————————————

Mary II
1662–94

When the Roman Catholic James II was driven from the English throne, it cost his elder daughter, Mary, married to Prince William of Orange, many heartsearchings concerning her duty: she accepted the crown jointly with her husband from Parliament, as she believed it was God's will that England should have Protestant rulers, but she never ceased to feel distress at her undutifulness as a daughter. Her life in England as Queen was full of anxieties, chiefly for her husband on his campaigns in Ireland or Flanders. She was sustained by her devout Anglicanism, but none the less all her surviving meditations give the reader the feeling of the immense strain which the search for what they thought of as rightful resignation to God's will imposed on sensitive seventeenth-century members of the Church of England. She died of smallpox in 1694, childless, which was a bitter grief to her, and leaving her husband whom she dearly loved and who was so shattered by her death that for a time his friends were frightened that he might die too. But he lived on for another seven years, building Greenwich Hospital in her memory, and refusing all suggestions of a second marriage: 'If you have forgotten your mistress, I have not.'

From a Meditation by the Queen written in February 1691:

Regard with an eye of compassion those who are in Ireland and if it is thy will put an end to that unhappy war. Bless to this end the efforts of our general Mr de Ginkle and the others who have been employed in this work. Give to them all that thou believest they have need of for an affair so grand and important, but above all bless my husband. I supplicate thee in all humility that his soul may remain among the living, preserve his person from all danger and harm. O my God, if it is thy will to finish the work thou hast commenced by him, preserve him to be between thy hands the instrument to bring peace to thy Zion and rebuild the walls of thy Jerusalem. O my God, regard not our sins, use us to the honour of thy great name and for thy mercy take care of thine anointed. Pardon me, thy unworthy servant, if I have been too persistent. I finish all with this resignation perfect that my Saviour hath taught and put himself in practice. Not my will but thine be done in all things.

55

Celia Fiennes
1662–1741

The granddaughter of the first Viscount Saye and Sele was born into a family who were devoted to the Parliamentary cause both before and during the Civil War – her three uncles, five uncles by marriage and her father all fought against the King. At the time of her birth and upbringing, as the Restoration had taken place, they were living unobtrusively on their estates but there can be no doubt as to their religious and political sympathies. However, it is not as a puritan spinster lady that Celia is remembered, but as an intrepid traveller. Her first long journey was to the north of England in 1697 for the good of her health, and after that she continued to make expeditions, from the interest of them as much as in the search for health, describing them in her journals. She went on horseback, attended by servants, and in spite of all the discomforts and even dangers of seventeenth-century travel she seems to have found real satisfaction and pleasure in these undertakings, going as far as Land's End in the west and Newcastle in the north, both immensely remote places then. She observed towns, manufactures, nature of the country and the many houses she visited or where she stayed.

In Cornwall she noted:

I heard a pretty good Sermon but that which was my greatest pleasure was the good Landlady I had; she was but an ordinary plaine woman but she was as understanding in the best things as most, the experience of reall religion and her quiet submission and self resignation to the will of God in all things, and especially in the placeing her in a remoteness, to the best advantages of hearing and being in such a publick employment which she desired and aimed at the discharging soe as to adorn the Gospel of her Lord and Saviour and the care of her children; indeed I was much pleased and edify'd by her conversation, and that pitch of soul resignation to the will of God, and thankfulness that God enabled and owned her therein, was an attainment few reach that have greater advantages of learning and knowing the mind of God; but this plainly led me to see that as God himself teacheth soe as none teacheth like him, soe he can discover himself to those immediately that have not the opportunity of seeing him in his sanctuary, and therefore to him we must address for help in this or any duty he calls us to, both in the use of what meanes he appoynts, as alsoe for success and blessing on it.

--------- 56 ---------

The Duke of Marlborough
1650–1722

John Churchill, first Duke of Marlborough, is one of the most mysterious characters of the late seventeenth and early eighteenth centuries. The brilliant general, the shrewd negotiator, the ambitious founder of a great tradition, the devoted husband of a fiery wife – all these were enclosed in the handsome person, behind the beautiful manners. But all the time there is a feeling that there is *more* to him, not revealed, not exposed. Many of his contemporaries seem to have been baffled, too: William III gave the impression of neither liking nor trusting him, but handed on his unfinished work for the defeat of Louis XIV to him, apparently with confidence that it would be completed. Winston Churchill, in his great *Life*, defends him vehemently, and cites evidence of the Duke's sincere religion.

After his victory over the French at the battle of Ramillies in 1706 Marlborough wrote to his wife:

I have appointed next Sunday for the army to return thanks to God for the protection He has been pleased to give us. For on this occasion it has been very visible, for the French had not only greater numbers than we, but all their best troops. I hope the Queen will appoint a speedy thanksgiving day at St Paul's, for the goodness of God is so very great that if He had suffered us to have been beaten, the liberties of all the allies had been lost.

--------------------------------- 57 ---------------------------------

William Law
1686–1761

William Law led a quiet and retired life as an Anglican clergyman who felt it wrong to take the oaths of allegiance to George I, as he believed that the Stuart claim to the throne was the rightful one. He wrote several immensely influential books, among them *A Serious Call to a Devout and Holy Life*, *The Spirit of Prayer* and *The Spirit of Love*. Among others, his work influenced the Wesleys, Johnson and Keble. He was greatly in favour of singing the psalms to oneself when alone – could that have affected Charles Wesley's hymn writing? William Law was renowned for his personal charities and his benevolence.

From *A Serious Call*:

Men of worldly business, therefore, must not look upon themselves as at liberty to live to themselves, to sacrifice to their own humours and tempers, because their employment is of a worldly nature. But they must consider that, as the world and all worldly professions as truly belong to God, as persons and things that are devoted to the altar, so it is as much the duty of men in worldly business to live wholly unto God, as it is the duty of those who are devoted to Divine service.

As the whole world is God's, so the whole world is to act for God . . . As all things are God's, so all things are to be used and regarded as the things of God. For men to abuse things on earth, and live to themselves, is the same rebellion against God as for angels to abuse things in Heaven; because God is just the same Lord of all on earth, as he is the Lord of all in Heaven.

Although, therefore, prayer does not consist in fine words, or studied expressions; yet as words speak to the soul, as they have a certain power of raising thoughts in the soul; so those words which speak of God in the highest manner, which most fully express the power and presence of God, which raise thoughts in the soul most suitable to the greatness and providence of God, are the most useful and edifying in our prayers.

58

Bishop Butler
1692–1752

Joseph Butler, Bishop of Bristol and then of Durham, was immensely influential through his learned works, of which the most famous was the *Analogy of Religion*, published in 1736, which had a great effect on believers in the following century. (Gladstone devoted much time and care to preparing an edition of Butler's works.) Butler had been brought up as a Presbyterian, but conformed to the Church of England which meant that he could go to Oxford, at that time closed to Freechurchmen. He was said to have declined the Archbishopric of Canterbury: his great aim seems to have been to convince people of the truth of religion by learned works and reasoned arguments – he had no tendency to grab preferment for himself. It was sad that when John Wesley preached to great effect in his diocese of Bristol he could not approve of what Wesley was doing; it was a complete difference in viewpoints.

From his sermon *Upon the Ignorance of Man*:

Thus the scheme of Providence, the ways and works of God, are too vast, of too large extent for our capacities. There is, as I may speak, such an expense of power, and wisdom, and goodness, in the formation and government of the world, as is too much for us to take in or comprehend. Power and wisdom and goodness are manifest to us in all those works of God which come within our view: but there are likewise infinite stores of each poured forth through the immensity of creation, no part of which can be thoroughly understood without taking in its reference and respect to the whole; and this is what we have not faculties for . . . so our ignorance should teach us that there may be reasons which originally made it fit that many things should be concealed from us which we have perhaps natural capacities for understanding; many things concerning the designs, methods and ends of Divine Providence in the government of the world . . . The Almighty may cast clouds and darkness round about him for reasons and purposes of which we have not the least glimpse or conception.

Butler was not an optimist, and on being appointed to the Bishopric of Durham (then a very wealthy and powerful post) he wrote to a friend words which express feelings which many bishops may have had in the past, but which now apply to others who find themselves in powerful positions: how to be at the same time in authority and keep one's conscience?

I thank you for your kind congratulations, though I am not without my doubts and fears how far the occasion of them is a real subject of congratulation to me . . . I foresee many difficulties in the station I am coming into, and no advantage worth thinking of, except some greater power of being serviceable to others; and whether this be an advantage entirely depends on the use one shall make of it. I pray God it may be a good one . . . this right use of fortune and power is more difficult than the generality of even good people think, and requires both a guard upon one's self, and strength of mind to withstand solicitations, greater, I wish I may not find it, than I am master of.

Butler had a serious and devout doctrine of the church:

Christ has a kingdom which is 'not of this world'. He founded a Church, to be to mankind a standing memorial of religion, and invitation to it; which He promised to be with always even to the end. He exercises an invisible government over it Himself, and by His Spirit: over that part of it, which is militant here on earth, a government of discipline, 'for the perfecting of the saints, for the edifying His body: till we are all come in the unity of the faith, and of the knowledge of the son of God, unto a perfect man, *unto the measure of the stature of the fulness of Christ'. Of this Church, all persons scattered over the world who live in obedience to His laws are members.*

A prayer which concluded a sermon on the love of our neighbours:

O Almighty God, inspire us with this divine principle (of love); kill in us all the seeds of envy and ill-will; and help us, by cultivating within ourselves the love of our neighbour, to improve in the love of Thee. Thou hast placed us in various kindreds, friendships and relations as the school of discipline for our affections; help us by the due exercise of them to improve to perfection, till all partial affection be lost in that entire universal one, and Thou, O God, shalt be all in all.

--- 59 ---

John Wesley
1703–91

The founder of Methodism himself dated his conversion in 1738, but long before that he had been earnestly seeking to do the will of God: it was 'Assurance' that seems to have come to him in that year. For the rest of his life he was incessant in evangelistic work – travelling many thousands of miles preaching, teaching, organizing, writing innumerable letters of help and counsel. He never left the Church of England: the separation of the Methodists was only completed after his death. All his life he fought courageously against the apathy and sin of the world, rising in the early hours to pray before his amazingly full days began.

Wesley's *Prayers for Wednesday Morning*:

O God, blessed for ever, we thank and praise Thee for all Thy benefits, for the comforts of this life, and our hope of everlasting salvation in the life to come.

Thou hast delivered Thine own Son for us all. How shalt Thou not with Him also freely give us all things?

We depend upon Thee, especially for the grace of Thy Holy Spirit. May we feel it perpetually bearing us up, by the strength of our most holy faith, above all the temptations that may at any time assault us.

Let Thy mighty power enable us to do our duty toward Thee and toward all men, with care, diligence, zeal, and perseverance unto the end. Help us to be meek and gentle in our conversation, prudent and discreet in ordering our affairs, observant of Thy fatherly providence in everything that befalls us, thankful for Thy benefits, patient under Thy chastisements, and readily disposed for every good word and work.

Deliver us, we beseech Thee, from worldly cares and foolish desires; from vain hopes and causeless fears; and so dispose our hearts that death itself may not be dreadful to us.

May our hearts be so firmly established in grace that nothing may affright us or shake our constancy.

We commend unto Thee all mankind. Bless our Sovereign, his counsellors and ministers and all employed in public business, whether spiritual or civil, that whatsoever they do may be for Thy glory and the public good.

Be gracious unto all that are near and dear to us, and keep us all in Thy fear and love. Guide us, good Lord, and govern us by the same Spirit, that we may be so united to Thee here as not to be divided when Thou art pleased to call us hence, but may together enter into Thy glory, through Jesus Christ, our blessed Lord and Saviour, who hath taught us when we pray to say: Our Father, etc.

It is thought that this was the last letter he ever wrote, in February, 1791, to support William Wilberforce in his struggle against the Slave Trade:

Balam, February 24, 1791.
Dear Sir, Unless the divine power has raised you up to be as Athanasius contra mundum, *I see not how you can go through your glorious enterprise in opposing that execrable villany, which is the scandal of religion, of England, and of human nature. Unless God has raised you up for this very thing, you will be worn out by the opposition of men and devils. But if God be for you, who can be against you? Are all of them together stronger than God? O be not weary of well doing! Go on, in the name of God and in the power of His might, till even American slavery (the vilest that ever saw the sun) shall vanish away before it . . .*

That He who has guided you from youth up may continue to strengthen you in this and all things is the prayer of, dear sir,
Your affectionate servant.

Charles Wesley
1707–88

Over five hundred of Charles Wesley's hymns are said to be still in use, out of the several thousand he composed, chiefly while travelling on horseback on his evangelistic journeys after his conversion in 1738. Like his brother John he travelled and preached and organized, and although some of their views were different they were united in fundamental aims and in close affection. Charles' legacy of hymns and singing heartily and reverently have been of immense importance in Methodist worship.

The following are extracts from one of his greatest hymns, *Wrestling Jacob*:

> *Come, O Thou Traveller unknown,*
> *Whom still I hold, but cannot see,*
> *My company before is gone,*
> *And I am left alone with Thee,*
> *With Thee all night I mean to stay*
> *And wrestle till the Break of Day.*
>
> *I need not tell Thee who I am,*
> *My Misery, or Sin declare,*
> *Thyself hast call'd me by my Name,*
> *Look on thy Hands, and read it there,*
> *But who, I ask Thee, who art Thou,*
> *Tell me thy Name, and tell me now?*
>
> *In vain Thou strugglest to get free,*
> *I never will unloose my Hold:*
> *Art Thou the Man that died for me?*
> *The Secret of thy Love unfold;*
> *Wrestling I will not let Thee go,*
> *Till I thy Name, thy Nature know.*

Yield to me Now – for I am weak;
  But confident in Self-despair:
Speak to my Heart, in Blessings speak,
  Be conquer'd by my Instant Prayer,
Speak, or Thou never hence shall move
And tell me if thy Name is Love.

I know Thee, Saviour, who Thou art,
  Jesus, the feeble Sinner's Friend;
Nor wilt Thou with the Night depart,
  But stay and love me to the End;
Thy Mercies never shall remove,
Thy Nature, and thy Name is Love.

61

Dr Johnson
1709–84

Samuel Johnson, who compiled the great Dictionary, was a convinced Christian and a deeply pious man. He himself said that he had been influenced by William Law's *A Serious Call to a Devout and Holy Life*. He was not only a believer, but was immensely charitable, supporting a group of difficult people even poorer than himself in his own house and bearing with their eccentricities and demands. His friend Mrs Thrale wrote of him: 'Johnson thought that God Almighty sent us here *to do* something – not merely to *stare about*.'

It was his custom to compose prayers for his own private use, and many have survived.

Written on his birthday in 1768:

Almighty and most merciful Father, Creator and Preserver of Mankind, look down with pity upon my troubles and maladies. Heal my body, strengthen my mind, compose my distraction, calm my inquietude, and relieve my terrours, that if it please Thee I may run the race that is set before me with peace, patience, constancy and confidence. Grant this, O Lord, and take not from me Thy Holy Spirit, but pardon and bless me for the sake of Jesus Christ our Lord. Amen.

Prayer concerning the Study of Religion:

Almighty God, our heavenly Father, without Whose help labour is useless, without Whose light search is vain, invigorate my studies and direct my enquiries, that I may, by due diligence and right discernment, establish myself and others in Thy holy faith. Take not, O Lord, Thy Holy Spirit from me, let not evil thoughts have domination in my mind. Let me not linger in ignorance, but enlighten and support me, for the Sake of Jesus Christ our Lord. Amen.

62

Sister Catherine Witham
1756

From the accession of Elizabeth I to the time of the French Revolution English Catholic women who wished to enter a convent had to travel overseas, as it was not possible to maintain Catholic monastic establishments in the very Protestant England of those years. The Bridgettine nuns settled in Lisbon in 1594, and continued there as an English community until 1861. (They are now back in England.) After the great Lisbon earthquake, one of the nuns, Kitty Witham, wrote home to reassure her mother. The following are extracts from her long letter, giving an account of the appalling disaster:

To be shure we was all in great danger; but Allmighty God's goodness spaird us, sweet Jesus make me and us all grateful to his devine Majesty for the great favour he has done us; . . . . I was washing up the tea things when the Dreadfull afair hapned. itt began like the rattleing of Coaches, and the things befor me danst up and downe upon the table, I look about me and see the Walls a shakeing and a falling down then I up and took to my heells, with Jesus in my mouth. . . . I mett with some of the good Nuns they Cryed Outt run to the low garden, I ask where the rest was, they sayde there, so Blessed be his holy Name we all mett together, and run no further, we was all as glad to see one another alive and well as can be exprest. We spent the day in prayers, but with a great deal of fear and aprehension, as we had shakes and trembles all that day and night. . . . but God's holy

Name be praised for spairing us, for there is some toons in Portugal that is quite swallowed up. This youll Read in the Newspapers, as allso a present from the good King of England to the King of Portugall, God bless him for itt, for tis Certainly Necessary for his subjects. The fleet is not yett come in but tis expected dayly. I wish an opportunity would offer for I have something to send you, for only God knows how long we have to live for I believe this world will not last long. happy are those that has gon well out of itt.

Mrs Edward Boscawen
1719–1805

In 1742 Fanny Evelyn married a naval officer, Edward Boscawen, who was to become one of England's greatest Admirals of the time of William Pitt the Elder and his wars against France. Many of her letters to her husband while he was at sea survive, and show how happy the marriage was. Hatchlands, in Surrey, which the Admiral and she built from his prize money and where she lived for many years, still exists and is now in the care of the National Trust. The Admiral died in 1761 and she never remarried, but retained her capacity for friendship and her tenderheartedness.

She was one of the best-liked and best-respected learned or 'blue-stocking' women of her day, the friend of others of similar tastes such as Mrs Montagu and Mrs Delaney. The letter given here was written to a friend who had just lost her mother.

> *Glan Villa.*
> *18th November, 1777.*
> *If compassion, if tenderest pity, or the most unfeigned sympathy could relieve your distress, my dearest friend, then indeed would your affliction be lessened. But this cannot be; nor indeed any other help, as yet, but that which you endeavour to lay hold of – Help from above. Time, the wretch's friend, will, more than you can now believe, skim over this bleeding wound, and take away the pain. Business (and more than one tender tie calls you to exert yourself) and friendship, which now soothes your grief, will contribute greatly to dispel it.*

All these, my dear Cousine, are remedies; slow ones, we must confess, nor can any take effect, except that greatest one of all – Christian resignation. 'Thy will be done' should go farther than the lips, and I suppose we are apt to believe it does, till we are tried, and then alas, how difficult do we find it to say heartily and sincerely 'not my will but Thine be done'; indeed this is beyond human strength in such sorrows as your's. Nor do the pious tears of filial affection offend our gracious Master, who shed them over his departed friend, and in compassion for those that lamented him, for He knoweth whereof we are made. He even experienced our infirmities, was a Man of Sorrows, and acquainted with grief.

I do entirely approve my dear child, of your remaining with your father, to whom all your duty will be transferred, and whose loss requires all your tenderness to alleviate, as indeed his constant kindness to you requires all your gratitude.

Your beloved mother has often assured me that you were without a fault towards her. Is not that a comfort inexpressible now, my dear friend, for were it otherwise the hour for repairing anything amiss is passed, never, alas, to be recalled.

But you have satisfaction to know that nothing was wanting on your side to make her (as she was, and as she deserved to be, dear soul) a most happy mother to the last moment of her life.

We wished, most earnestly wished, that it had pleased God to have granted her a longer one in this world; but how know we what pains she would have suffered, what misery endur'd. No, my dear friend; we are ignorant and blind, but our gracious Master is All-knowing and All-wise. To him let us dutifully submit: on Him let us humbly confide.

Adieu. God bless and comfort you,

F.B.

64

Samuel Whitbread

1720–91

Samuel Whitbread (the father of the famous reformer, another Samuel) was apprenticed to a London brewer at the age of sixteen. Later he founded the famous Whitbread's brewery in Chiswell Street, in the City of London, which still exists and whose famous horses still pull the drays. Even though he had little education he was a successful pioneer in the use of steam machinery – he seems to have been the best kind of 'self-made' man: original, hardworking, charitable and full of initiative. He became MP for Bedford town in 1768, he was a friend of Pitt and knew Dr Johnson and owned a copy of Dr Johnson's *Prayers and Meditations*. As a devout man he composed his own prayers, and this one was written on his seventy-first birthday:

I bless thee O God for all thy goodness to all my dear dear dear children. . . . Oh may I never forget my God, beware of covetousness and be mindful of the wants of others and never turn my face from any poor man that the face of God may never be turned from me . . . I pray for opportunity to take leave of my dear children and recommend them to the mercy and favour of God and advise them against waste of time especially in bed as incompatible with duty to God and man.

65

William Pitt the Younger
1759–1806

The young man who became George III's Prime Minister at only twenty-four years old could be chilly and shy in public, but his close friends were devoted to him, and amongst them was William Wilberforce, also a young MP and the campaigner against the Slave Trade. When Wilberforce experienced an Evangelical conversion in 1785 he wrote to Pitt and told him about it, explaining that although he hoped to be able to support Pitt as he had done earlier, yet 'I could no more be so much a party man as I had been before' – expressing, in fact, his belief that religion must now take priority over everything. Pitt wrote a long letter back, of which the following are extracts:

. . . You will not suspect me of thinking lightly of any moral or religious motives which guide you. As little will you believe that I think your understanding or judgment easily misled. But forgive me if I cannot help expressing my fear that you are nevertheless deluding yourself into principles which have but too much tendency to counteract your own object, and to render your virtues and your talents useless both to yourself

and mankind. I am not, however, without hopes that my anxiety paints this too strongly. For you confess that the character of religion is not a gloomy one, and it is not that of an enthusiast. But why then this preparation of solitude, which can hardly avoid tincturing the mind either with melancholy or with superstition? If a Christian may act in the several relations of life, must he seclude himself from all to become so? Surely the principles as well as the practice of Christianity are simple, and lead not to meditation only but to action.

Pitt was quite right about his friend – Wilberforce's evangelicalism sustained him through years of campaigning against the trade of buying slaves in West Africa and selling them in America and the West Indies, and against the institution of slavery itself. The friendship between the two men continued, but Pitt never came to share Wilberforce's evangelical beliefs.

66

Admiral Lord Nelson
1758–1805

Horatio, Viscount Nelson possessed a very complex nature: there was the good friend, the beloved officer, the naval genius – but there was also the other side, the capacity for vanity and self-deception. Yet under all the complications of character and experience was the son of the Norfolk vicarage, the man found on his knees in his cabin before the Battle of Trafalgar (where he was to meet his death) who had just written the following prayer:

May the Great God whom I worship grant to my Country, and for the benefit of Europe in general, a great and glorious Victory; and may no misconduct in any one tarnish it; and may humanity after Victory be the predominant feature in the British Fleet. For myself, individually, I commit my life to Him who made me, and may His blessing light upon my endeavours for serving my Country faithfully. To Him I resign myself and the just cause which is entrusted to me to defend.

William Wilberforce
1759–1833

The man who worked so long and so hard for the suppression
of the trade in slaves and for the abolition of slavery itself, was
also a leader of the Evangelical Movement. That movement, at
the end of the eighteenth and into the nineteenth century,
stretched across various denominations and was characterized
by individualism, an intense seriousness, an awareness of the
individual's relationship with God and co-operation in certain
great campaigns (such as the founding of the Church
Missionary Society and the Bible Society). Sometimes it
resulted in great works greatly done, sometimes it provoked
violent reactions (because of what many considered its habit of
interfering with everyone and everything and a certain
propensity for making hard judgments). Sometimes people
just did not wish to have their attention drawn to terrible evils.
The descendants of Wilberforce's contemporaries often kept
the seriousness and the capacity for endeavour but developed
different views on the church and social policy. It is a subject of
infinite complexity, but certainly Wilberforce represents it
well; only, as an MP and someone welcome in society, he had a
broader knowledge of worldly life than many Evangelicals –
including his own wife, who was of the most serious nature.
The following letter of 1804 is addressed by Wilberforce to Miss
Hannah More, the philanthropist and pioneer of Sunday
Schools:

My dear Friend,

*Though I have not written to you, you have often been in our thoughts
and mouths. We heard with concern of your having suffered much
pain . . . It is, however, an unspeakable consolation under all trials of
every sort to reflect that they do not happen by chance, nor merely from the
effect of general laws which, in their gigantic rotation, crush a few more or*

less of the insignificant beings who chance to be under them; such a way of talking about general laws is a most saddening system, and of an atheistical complexion . . . How much more healing is it to consider that all which befalls is specifically and individually ordained for us by Him who combines infinite goodness with Almighty wisdom and power, who afflicts not his creatures needlessly, much less those who fear and love Him, and wait on Him, and who has assured us that all shall finally work together for our good. I shall not apologize to you for pouring forth all this commonplace stuff. In truth it is these commonplace positions that are one's daily bread – one's support and comfort.

68

Sydney Smith
1771–1845

Sydney Smith's reputation as a wit has tended to overshadow his hard work as a country clergyman before he finally became a Canon of St Paul's Cathedral. At a time when the majority of the Anglican clergy were suffering from the reaction of fearful Toryism against the French Revolution and were suspicious of all change, he gave great service to the Whig cause by his speaking and writing and support of reform. He wrote of himself in 1835: 'I began attacking abuses thirty or forty years ago, when it was almost safer to be a felon than a Reformer.'

This particular letter shows his sympathy with depression, but he was also a great advocate for a clergyman knowing something of medicine, and he prescribed for and treated illnesses in his remote parishes. Lady Georgiana, who was the daughter of the famous Georgiana, Duchess of Devonshire and who lived at Castle Howard, must have been able to get the best medical advice of the time, but she was clearly turning to Sydney Smith for comfort:

Dear Lady Georgiana,
. . . Nobody has suffered more from low spirits than I have done – so I feel for you. 1st. Live as well as you dare. 2nd. Go into the shower-bath

with a small quantity of water at a temperature low enough to give you a slight sensation of cold, 75° or 80°. 3rd. Amusing books. 4th. Short views of human life – not further than dinner or tea. 5th. Be as busy as you can. 6th. See as much as you can of those friends who respect and like you. 7th. And of those acquaintances who amuse you. 8th. Make no secret of low spirits to your friends, but talk of them freely – they are always worse for dignified concealment. 9th. Attend to the effects tea and coffee produce upon you. 10th. Compare your lot with that of other people. 11th. Don't expect too much from human life – a sorry business at the best. 12th. Avoid poetry, dramatic representations (except comedy), music, serious novels, melancholy sentimental people, and everything likely to excite feeling or emotion not ending in active benevolence. 13th. Do good, and endeavour to please everybody of every degree. 14th. Be as much as you can in the open air without fatigue. 15th. Make the room where you commonly sit, gay and pleasant. 16th. Struggle by little and little against idleness. 17th. Don't be too severe upon yourself, or underrate yourself, but do yourself justice. 18th. Keep good blazing fires. 19th. Be firm and constant in the exercise of rational religion. 20th. Believe me, dear Lady Georgiana,

Very truly yours,
Sydney Smith

———————— 69 ————————

Jane Austen
1775–1817

There are problems of conduct and morality, searchingly dissected, in all Jane Austen's novels, but very little discussion of religion or spirituality: her reserve was deep on these subjects. In *Mansfield Park*, however, there is a short but very significant description of why two young women who had been taught what was right did not act upon it: the reason given is that they had never been required to put their religion 'into practice'. From what we know of her own life, Jane Austen herself *did* put her religion into practice and her family bore witness to this in what they had inscribed on her grave in Winchester Cathedral:

In Memory of
JANE AUSTEN
youngest daughter of the late
Revd GEORGE AUSTEN
*formerly Rector of Steventon in this County
she departed this Life on the 18th of July, 1817,
aged 41, after a long illness supported with
the patience and the hopes of a Christian.*

*The benevolence of her heart,
the sweetness of her temper, and
the extraordinary endowments of her mind
obtained the regard of all who knew her and
the warmest love of her intimate connections.
Their grief is in proportion to their affection
they know their loss to be irreparable,
but in their deepest affliction they are consoled
by a firm though humble hope that her chairty,
devotion, faith and purity have rendered
her soul acceptable in the sight of her*
REDEEMER.

70

The Marchioness of Anglesey
1781–1853

The Marquess of Anglesey, who was thought to be the finest cavalry leader of his day and who fought and lost a leg at Waterloo, had eloped some years earlier with a sister-in-law of the Duke of Wellington: very complicated divorce proceedings had ensued, as both parties were married, but in the end they were free and able to marry each other. Lady Anglesey must have suffered deeply, as the treatment given to any divorced woman by society in the early nineteenth century was liable to be cold and unkind, and even her husband's heroism, public services and popularity did not completely protect her. Also, as the following letter makes clear, she was a believer and was impelled to write to her husband in 1850 showing how the events of forty years before had remained with her:

We have both been mercifully preserved through a length of years beyond the usual allotment to man, & I sincerely hope that you may still be preserved for the sake of many to whom your existence is of such importance! My own life is of little use to any Body – but time must be short for us both, & life fast dying away, & our latter days can only be valuable to ourselves as giving us a longer period for preparation to meet our Heavenly Father . . . It is a solemn subject for us to reflect on by-gone days, past to us as if they had never been, but not so with God; in his memory every sin is recorded, and to him we must ere long give an account of all our deeds as if he were in ignorance – This we are distinctly told in his holy word, but in that blessed Book we are as clearly promised perfect forgiveness if we approach him deeply humbled under a sense of our sins – I feel certain that you go with me now in these things, altho' we may differ upon more trifling points our hopes and dependence rest entirely in our Saviour; without his mediation and death what would have become of us?

If it should please God to take me first I am sure that my dying moment will be soothed by the reflexions which your present state of mind affords me, & I pray God that you may go on daily advancing in holiness, for there is need for improvement in all of us! We have all the same means given by which alone we can be carried forward, & in the end obtain what we ask for – the Kingdom of Heaven – There I trust my dearest we shall be reunited.

71

Lady Caroline Lamb
1785–1828

Much has been written about Lady Caroline Lamb and her husband William, later Lord Melbourne and Queen Victoria's first Prime Minister. Lady Caroline's unconventional nature, her relationship with Byron, her wild behaviour and the publication of her novel *Glenarvon* with its thinly covered caricatures of her friends and enemies have all been examined at length. What has been less stressed is her patience, gentleness and change of heart in her last illness.

She wrote to her sister-in-law in December 1827:

I consider my painful illness as a great blessing. I feel return'd to my God & my duty & my dearest husband, & my heart which was so proud &

insensible is quite overcome with the great kindness I receive. I brought myself to be quite another person & broke that horrid spell which prevented my saying my prayers; so that if I were better, I would go with you & your dear children to church. I say all this, dearest Maria, lest you should think I flew to religion because I was in danger – it is no such thing, my heart is softened, I see how good and kind others are & I am quite resigned to die – I do not myself think there is a chance for me.

Sir Harry Smith
1787–1860

One of the young officers of the Light Division under Wellington in the Peninsular War, Brigade-Major Harry Smith, rescued a Spanish girl of not quite fourteen years old, Juana de Leon, after the sack of Badajoz in 1812. They were married three days later and from then onwards she went with him everywhere, up to and almost including his battles, through Spain, France, the Waterloo campaign, India and South Africa (where the town of Ladysmith is named after her). It is one of the greatest and lifelong English love stories. In his *Autobiography* he wrote:

Thus, as good may come out of evil, this scene of devastation and spoil yielded to me a treasure invaluable; to me who, among so many dear friends, had escaped all dangers; to me, a wild youth not meriting such reward, and, however desirous, never able to express half his gratitude to God Almighty for such signal marks of His blessing shown to so young and so thoughtless a being. From that day to this she has been my guardian angel. She has shared with me the dangers and privations, the hardships and fatigues, of a restless life of war in every quarter of the globe. No murmur has ever escaped her. Bereft of every relative, of every tie to her country but the recollection of it, united to a man of different though Christian religion, yet that man has been and is her all, on whom have hinged the closed portals of hope, happiness and bliss; if opened, misery, destitution and bereavement, and every loss language can depict summed up in one word, 'He is lost to me.' But, O my God, Thou hast kindly spared us to each other; we have, through Thy grace, been but little separated, and we have, in union of soul, received at Thy holy altar the Blessed Sacrament of the Body and Blood of Christ. May we, through His mediation, be still spared to each other in this life, and in the life to come be eternally united in Heaven!

73

Lady Lyttelton
1787–1870

Sarah Spencer was daughter of the Earl Spencer who was First Lord of the Admiralty in Nelson's day, sister to the Lord Althorp who did so much to achieve the passing of the 1832 Reform Bill, and cousin to Lady Caroline Lamb, and so grew up in the heart of Whig society. As the wife of the third Lord Lyttelton she was a great influence on the whole mid-Victorian Lyttelton clan, all notable for cheerfulness, cleverness and humble piety. In her widowhood she became governess for eight years to Queen Victoria's children and her letters form an interesting commentary on the early Victorian court. She was a woman who inspired great trust and affection.

A letter of 20 August 1853 on the problems of elderly women:

Dearest Lady Pembroke, At least I can thank you with some knowledge of the subject for 'Things to be Thought of' which I have read with great pleasure. It was so kind of you to think of sending it to me. I only wish I got any lasting good from such pleasant advice! One other wish I have. That someone would get at the author and induce her to write a few lectures to old ladies. I feel that we are always sadly neglected by good-book writers, and I fancy this lady might know how to help us . . . when one's heart, from having been in its best days made of kid, becomes a bit of hard old leather, and having been always at a low temperature, cools down into a sadly chilly and dreary state, something might do good. I never find anything fit for me. It is tiresome to be told 'not to be too fond of this world,' and 'not to be anxious for pleasure and amusement,' and 'to endure loneliness and dulness and silence' when all I want is to love more, *and to smile* more, *and to be* more *amused and* more *merry, and less poky and morose and dry and grave!*

John Keble

1792–1866

The publication in 1828, of *The Christian Year*, a book of poems on the Book of Common Prayer, first made Keble known to a wide public, but it was his famous Assize Sermon on 'National Apostasy' in 1833 which marked the start of the 'Oxford Movement', so called because most of its leaders were dons at Oxford, or the 'Tractarian Movement' because they made their opinions known through a famous series of tracts. This Movement aimed to bring back life and devoutness to the Church of England, which in many places had become dry and out of touch with its history as well as with its mission. Keble remained faithful to this ideal of an Apostolic Church of England all his life and tried to carry out what he felt to be the duty of a country parson in his parish at Hursley, near Winchester. He was the close friend and associate of Newman, Pusey and other members of the Oxford Movement, and when Newman was converted to Roman Catholicism in 1845 those who remained Anglican looked more and more to Keble for guidance. Keble had several times referred to the church as an ark, and the meaning of the symbol must have come home to him in the years of difficulty. These lines from the 'Evening Hymn' in *The Christian Year* are very famous:

> *Thou Framer of the light and dark*
> *Steer through the tempest Thine own ark:*
> *Amid the howling wintry sea*
> *We are in port if we have Thee.*

It is a mistake to think that the first generation of the Oxford Movement were innovators in ceremonial observances – they were not interested in candles and incense, they were interested in the frequency, regularity and reverence with which services should be conducted. They had a high value for quietness, strictness and reserve in religious behaviour. Keble had written in the preface to *The Christian Year*:

Next to a sound rule of faith, there is nothing of so much consequence as a sober standard of feeling in matters of practical religion: and it is the peculiar happiness of the Church of England to possess, in her authorized formularies, an ample and secure provision for both. But in times of much leisure and unbounded curiosity, when excitement of every kind is sought after with a morbid eagerness, this part of the merit of our Liturgy is likely in some measure to be lost on many even of its sincere admirers: the very tempers which most require such discipline setting themselves, in general, most decidedly against it.

When Newman wrote to Keble in 1845 to tell him of his conversion, Keble replied in a long letter, of which this is an extract:

My dear Newman, you have been a kind and helpful friend to me in a way which scarce anyone else could have been, and you are so mixed up in my mind with old and dear and sacred thoughts, that I cannot well bear to part with you, most unworthy as I know myself to be; and yet I cannot go along with you. I must cling to the belief that we are not really parted – you have taught me so, and I scarce think you can unteach me – and, having relieved my mind with this little word I will only say God bless you and reward you a thousandfold all your help in every way to me unworthy and to so many others. May you have peace where you are gone, and help us in some way to get peace; but somehow I scarce think it will be in the way of controversy. And so, with somewhat of a feeling as if the Spring had been taken out of my year, I am always your affectionate and grateful J. Keble.

75

Queen Adelaide
1792–1849

The wife of William IV was abused by many people at the time of the Reform Bill agitation in 1832, because it was said that she was a reactionary Tory and was influencing the King against the Whig ministry and the Bill. What becomes clear in reading about her, however, is not what she may or may not have said privately about the Bill through nervousness concerning reform, but rather her general goodness and kindness. Coming from the small court of Saxe-Coburg Meiningen to Regency England cannot have been easy, and she was confronted by her husband's ten illegitimate children whom she treated with kindness. But perhaps her real unselfishness and magnanimity showed itself even more in her attitude to her niece Victoria, as Princess and then Queen – Queen Adelaide had lost her own children who would have inherited the crown, but she gave Victoria love and respect and her reward came in the consideration and affection with which Victoria responded (though not to the extent of church building as requested here).

From a letter to Queen Victoria of 1838, from Malta (Queen Adelaide was cruising in the Mediterranean):

My dearest Niece, The English mail going today gives me another opportunity to address you, and to name a subject to you which I think deserves your consideration, and about which I feel most anxious. It is the want of a Protestant Church in this place which I mean. There are so many English residents here, it is the seat of an English Government and there is not one church belonging to the Church of England . . . The consequence of this want of church accommodation has been that the Dissenters have established themselves in considerable numbers, and one cannot blame persons for attending their meetings when they have no church of their own.

I address myself to you, as the Head of the Church of England, and entreat you to consider well this important subject, and to talk it over with your Ministers and the Archbishop, in order to devise the best means of remedying a want so discreditable to our country. Should there be no funds at your disposal to effect this object, most happy shall I feel to contribute to any subscription which may be set on foot, and I believe that a considerable sum may be raised amongst the Protestants of this island, where all parties are most anxious to see a proper place of divine worship erected; without assistance from England, however, it cannot be effected.

In the end Queen Adelaide arranged for the erection of the church, and paid for it herself, at a cost of £10,000.

Thomas Arnold
1795–1842

Thomas Arnold is remembered as a great headmaster of Rugby and as the father of Matthew Arnold. What is less stressed is his tremendous interest in reform, not only in the school but in the church. He caused anxiety to fellow clergy by the liberalism of his religious ideas, just as he caused worry to some of the more conservative neighbours of Rugby School because of the same tendencies in politics. His exact contribution to nineteenth-century education will probably always be argued about, but there can be no doubt that he felt the first and greatest aim of a public school education was to teach the boys to grow up to be men who would love and serve God and who would use their talents and their capacity for hard work rightly.

A prayer which he used every day for the Sixth Form:

O Lord, who by Thy holy Apostle has taught us to do all things in the name of the Lord Jesus and to Thy glory, give Thy blessing, we pray Thee, to this our daily work, that we may do it in faith, and heartily, as unto the Lord and not unto men. All our powers of body and mind are Thine, and we would fain devote them to Thy service. Sanctify them and the work in which they are engaged; let us not be slothful, but fervent in spirit, and do Thou, O Lord, so bless our efforts that they may bring forth in us the fruits of true wisdom. Strengthen the faculties of our minds and dispose us to exert them, but let us always remember to exert them for Thy glory, and for the furtherance of Thy kingdom, and save us from all pride, vanity, and reliance upon our own power or wisdom. Teach us to seek after truth and enable us to gain it: but grant that we may ever speak the truth in love:— that while we know earthly things, we may know Thee and be known by Thee, through and in Thy Son, Jesus Christ. Give us this day Thy Holy Spirit, that we may be Thine in body and spirit in all our work and all our refreshments, through Jesus Christ Thy Son, our Lord, Amen.

The Earl of Shaftesbury
1801–85

There is a long list of good causes to which Antony
Ashley-Cooper devoted his life: children in the coal mines,
homeless people in the slums, the shortening of hours of work
in factories, the chimney sweep boys, the uncared-for lunatics
and countless other sufferers. He once wrote:

*When I feel old age creeping upon me and know that I must soon die – I
hope it is not wrong to say it – I cannot bear to leave this world with all the
misery in it.*

He was very happily married to Minnie Cowper, daughter of
the beautiful Emily Cowper who married the famous Lord
Palmerston after her widowhood in middle age. The difference
of opinions and attitudes in the family must have been
fantastic: Palmerston and his wife were of the Regency
generation, robust, worldly, sophisticated, living in the heart
of Society. Shaftesbury was deeply, even puritanically
Evangelical in religion, unworldly, outspoken, devoted to the
causes to which he felt he had been called by God. Great
gentleness and sensitivity on both sides must have been
exerted to preserve family harmony and it is immensely to
Palmerston's credit that he, who had been often considered as
a young man to be very abrasive, selfish and brash, managed to
allow for Shaftesbury's sensitivities.

When Palmerston was dying at the age of eighty-one, after
an idyllically happy marriage, Lady Palmerston summoned
Shaftesbury – she had collapsed in grief as the doctors had told
her there was no hope. She asked Shaftesbury to pray for her
husband. 'Ah, have I not during many years prayed for you
both, every morning and every night?' was the reply. 'Then
pray with me now,' she begged of him, and this Shaftesbury

faithfully did, both with her and her husband. It was the younger, the believing generation, coming to the help of the old.

— 78 —

Cardinal Newman
1801–90

John Henry Newman, one of the leaders of the Anglican Tractarian movement in Oxford, was converted to Roman Catholicism in 1845. His conversion was remarkable: it came not through discussions with Catholics or influence from them, but purely through the intellectual and spiritual effect of his studies of the early church, which convinced him gradually, over a long period, of the truth and orthodoxy of that church's position. His greatest work is his *Apologia pro Vita Sua*, written after his conversion, but long before that time he was famous for his sermons, his scholarship and his capacity for making disciples. Much later in the century Cosmo Gordon Lang wrote of his own time at the University Church of St Mary, Oxford, where Newman had worked and preached before he left Anglicanism:

The thought of John Henry Newman was seldom absent from me, whether I was celebrating at his altar or preaching from the pulpit from which he spoke. There were very few traditions about him among the parishioners. But one old lady remembered him vividly and said to me – and I thought it very significant: 'He used to wear a very shabby surplice, but when he read the lessons he seemed to be in Heaven.'

Professor J. G. Shairp, a friend of William Temple, was an admirer like him of Newman's sermons:

Those who had never heard Newman might fancy that his sermons would generally be about Apostolical Succession, or rights of the Church, or against Dissenters. Nothing of the kind. You might hear him preach for weeks without an allusion to these things. What there was of High Church teaching was implied rather than enforced . . . After hearing these sermons you might come away, still not believing the tenets peculiar to the High Church system; but you would be harder than most men if you did not feel more than ever ashamed of coarseness, selfishness, worldliness; if you did not feel the things of faith brought closer to the soul.

From Newman's own writings:

One gains nothing by sitting still. I am sure the Apostles did not sit still.

79

The Earl of Beaconsfield
1804–81

Gladstone spoke of Benjamin Disraeli, Earl of Beaconsfield, in his memorial oration, with the intuition which greatness shows to greatness however antagonistic, and said that one of his characteristics was 'his great Parliamentary courage'. The truth of this had been displayed by Disraeli's attitude towards his own Jewishness. He had been baptized as a boy of twelve, in consequence of his father's dispute with their synagogue. The Jews had not been emancipated then: Disraeli had nothing to gain and everything to lose by helping them in their struggle and by emphasizing his descent. He did both – he unflinchingly stood out for right and justice despite the embarrassment of his Tory squire followers. All through his life, through such difficulties, disappointments, frustrations and hazards as have afflicted few Victorian Prime Ministers, Disraeli displayed that continual self-mastery and lack of repining. It was Bismark who said of him: 'Der alte Jude – das ist der Mann!', but those who knew him best would have agreed without reservation.

His memoirs, from which the following quotations are taken, give the rich flavour of his idiosyncrasies – though not, perhaps, as richly as his novels, where several clerics are handled with feline skill. But for all the cynicism which he could show, his belief in the faith he was pushed into as a boy seems to have been absolutely genuine, if extremely individual.

Elmley (a friend of Disraeli's) was always saying, 'What did Jesus do before he was thirty? My conviction is that he must have had an eventful youth and that he travelled a great deal.' This travelling of Jesus was a great point with Elmley. He frequently recurred to it. I never could agree with him. It seemed such an original mind; so completely formed in seclusion, and with all its Shakespearean genius so essentially local. All the illustrations are drawn from inward resources, or from surrounding scenery.

'Of one Semitic nation, the Jews,' I observed, 'it can be said, that they invented alike the Ten Commandments & the Lord's Prayer.'

Richard Cobden
1804–65

It is a tribute to the House of Commons that, when Richard Cobden died, it was Disraeli, who had been fiercely opposed to his policy of repealing the Corn Laws with their import tax on food, who praised him most eloquently. The battle against the import taxes in the 1830s and 1840s had been jointly led by Cobden and Bright, and after Sir Robert Peel abolished these taxes the characters of both men came to be appreciated in Parliament as well as among the poor for whom they were struggling. It is difficult for later generations to imagine the acute distress of working people in the pre-repeal time: whatever subsequent English economic difficulties may have developed from free trade, certainly repeal was the only right measure at the time. At the height of the distress, in February 1841, a Manchester clergyman asked Cobden, who was an Anglican, to contribute to the building of ten new churches. Part of his reply was as follows:

The first and most pressing claim of the poor is for food: all other wants are secondary to this. It is in vain to try and elevate the moral and religious character of a people whose physical condition is degraded by the privation of the first necessaries of life; and hence we are told to pray for 'our daily bread' before spiritual graces. There is a legislative enactment which pre-

vents the poor of this town from obtaining a sufficiency of wholesome food, and I am sure the law only requires to be understood by our clergy to receive their unanimous condemnation. Surely a law of this kind must be denounced by the ministers of the Gospel. So convinced am I that there is no other mode of raising the condition of the working classes in the scale of morality or religion, whilst they are denied by Act of Parliament a sufficiency of food, that I have set apart as much of my income as I can spare from other claims for the purpose of effecting the abolition of the Corn Law and Provision Law. It is for this reason that I am reluctantly obliged to decline to contribute to the fund for building ten new churches. My course is, I submit, in strict harmony with the example afforded us by the divine author of Christianity, who preached upon the mountain and in the desert, beneath no other roof than the canopy of heaven, and who yet, we are told, was careful to feed the multitude that flocked around him.

Frederick Denison Maurice
1805–72

The influence Maurice exerted – and still exerts, whether directly or indirectly – is amazing: his contributions to theology, to reform, to Christian Socialism, to education and to genuine personal devotion were all of great and lasting importance.

He was born the son of a Unitarian minister, but became an Anglican and was ordained in 1834. By his preaching and teaching he roused the consciences of many to the unnecessary inequalities and cruelties of Victorian England. He was a supporter of co-operative and trade associations, a socialist, an advocate of votes for women and tireless in helping them to educational and social emancipation. (For example, helping to found Queen's College for women in 1847.) His *Theological Essays* of 1853 were thought to be dangerous and led to his dismissal from his Professorship of Divinity at King's College, London. He became Principal of the Working Men's College, of which he was a founder, and then went to Cambridge in 1866 as Professor of Moral Philosophy and stayed there until his death. During all these undertakings he continued to preach and his sermons display many of his beliefs.

When he wrote to his father as a young man to explain why he had joined the Church of England, he said he felt that human beings longed for a reconciliation between a mysterious and infinite God and one who could be known and understood:

If this be the one cry of human nature in all ages, just in proportion as it was enlightened, then cannot any explanation be found for it except only that which will satisfy it. If the Infinite Incomprehensible Jehovah is manifested in the person of a Man, a Man conversing with us, living among us, entering into all our infirmities and temptations, and passing into all our conditions, it is satisfied; if not, it remains unsatisfied. Man is still dealing with an incomprehensible Being, without any mode of comprehending Him. He may be revealed to him as his lawgiver, his sovereign, but he has no means of knowing Him as a friend.

Cardinal Manning
1808–92

Cardinal Manning was regarded as the most powerful of all the great Victorian Catholic prelates, through his great ability, his strong will and his close links with the Vatican. He had been an Anglican clergyman, who married young, but after his wife died he was desperately perturbed by the religious disagreements of the 1840s and was converted in 1851. He soon became very influential, being appointed Archbishop of Westminster in 1865, and Cardinal in 1875. He was a strong supporter of the Papacy and in the confidence of Pius IX and never hesitated to campaign against people who queried the decisions and powers of the Pope. In social matters he was immensely charitable and tireless in his work for the poor, and for conciliation in trade disputes. (For example, he supported the cause of the casual labourers in the docks and the agricultural labourers.)

Cardinal Vaughan described the end of his life:

I was by his bedside; he looked round to see that we were alone; he fumbled under the pillow for something; he drew out a battered little pocket-book full of a woman's fine handwriting. He said: 'For years you have been a son to me, Herbert; I know not to whom else to leave this – I leave it to you. Into this little book my dearest wife wrote her prayers and meditations. Not a day has passed, since her death, on which I have not prayed and meditated from this book. All the good I may have done, all the good I may have been, I owe to her. Take precious care of it.'

———— 83 ————

William Ewart Gladstone
1809–98

William Gladstone was not only a statesman and orator, but a profoundly learned Anglican. He had moved from the Evangelicalism of his parents to a different view of the church and was the friend and correspondent of many of the Tractarians. He was exceptional amongst Prime Ministers for the special care he took over church appointments and for the high quality of his nominees. He married Catherine Glynne, a remarkable woman of deep piety and compassion and a pioneer in much to do with hospitals, convalescent homes and orphanages.

The following is part of a correspondence he had with his wife in the early days of their marriage, when she was unhappy that political claims meant that they had so little time together:

. . . there is a speech in the third canto of the Paradiso of Dante, spoken by a certain Piccarda, which is a rare gem. I will only quote this one line:
In la sua voluntate e nostra pace.
The words are few and simple yet they appear to me to have an inexpressible majesty of truth about them as if they were spoken from the very mouth of God . . . The final state which we are to contemplate with hope and to seek by discipline is that in which our will shall be one with the will of God; not merely shall submit to it, not merely shall follow after it, but shall live and move with it even as the pulse of the blood in the extremities acts with the central movement of the heart. And this is to be obtained through a double

process; the first, that of checking, repressing, quelling, the inclination of the will to act with reference to self as a centre – that is, to mortify it; the second, to cherish, exercise and expand, its new and heavenly power of acting according to the will of God, first, perhaps, by painful effort in great feebleness and with many inconsistencies, but with continually augmenting regularity and force until obedience become a necessity of second nature.

And these two processes are carried on together. Your abundant overflowing affection as a wife leads you to wish we were together, while duty keeps us apart. You check that affection, school and subdue it – that is mortifying the individual will. That of itself is much more than the whole of what is contemplated by popular opinion as a Christian duty, for resignation is too often conceived to be merely a submission not unattended with complaint to what we have no power to avoid; but it is less than the whole of the work of a Christian. Your full triumph, as far as that particular occasion of duty is concerned, will be to find that you not merely repress outward complaint – nay, not merely repress inward tendencies to murmur – but that you would not if you could alter what in any manner God has plainly willed; that you have a satisfaction and a comfort in it because it is His will, although from its own native taste you would have revolted. Here is the great work of religion; here is the path through which sanctity is attained, the highest sanctity. And yet it is a path evidently to be traced in the course of our daily duties; for it is clear that the occasions of every day are numberless amidst the diversities of events upon which a true spiritual discrimination may find employment in discerning the will of God, and in which also the law of love and self-denial may be applied in the effort to conform to it both inwardly and outwardly so soon as it shall have been discerned. And thus the high attainments that have their crown and their reward in heaven do not require, in order that we may learn them, that we should depart from our common duties, but they lie by the wayside of life; and every pilgrim of this world may, if he have grace, become an adept in them.

When we are thwarted in the exercise of some innocent, laudable and almost sacred affection, as in the case, though its scale be small, out of which all this has grown, Satan has us at an advantage; because when the obstacle occurs we have a sentiment that the feeling baffled is a right one, and in indulging a rebellious temper we flatter ourselves that we are merely, as it were indignant on behalf, not of ourselves, but of a duty which we have been interrupted in performing. But our duties can take care of themselves when God calls us away from any of them, and when He interrupts the discharge of one it is to ascertain, by the manner of bearing the interruption, whether we are growing fit for another which is higher. To be able to relinquish a duty upon command shows a higher grace than to *be able to give up a mere pleasure for a duty; it shows a more practical discernment of the Divine will to distinguish between two things differing only in measure than between one which has a manifest stamp of God upon it and another which is but remotely related to Him, or what is commonly (and hazardously) called indifferent.*

'Such a beautiful letter this morning to thank you for,' ran Catherine's reply, 'a letter which I shall love to read again. What advantages I have in such a dear old man who is always showing me the right way in which to walk; indeed I am frightened to think what I ought to be.' To the casual or frivolous reader Gladstone's letter inevitably appears pompous and stilted, a curious document for a husband to write to a wife. It is indeed a curious letter, not because it shows so little affection or understanding but because it presupposes so much of both these qualities. Very few husbands, and certainly very few husbands as busy as William Gladstone, pay their wives the compliment of treating their complaints with complete seriousness. It would have been far easier to write a few loving phrases, hinting gently that after all Catherine had not so very much to grumble at but praising rather than blaming the devotion that could not bear even a temporary parting. Far easier, but it would have given no lasting answer to a question that was bound to grow in importance with the years as the pressure of public business on the one hand and the cares of a growing family on the other combined to make their enforced separations more and more frequent.

Instead, William Gladstone presented Catherine with the key to a philosophy by which to rule her whole life; and he answered it by reference to 'the foundation of all mental thoughts and acts, and the measure to which the whole experience of life inward and outward is referred'. To complain that he preached instead of comforting is to miss the whole point; he respected her too much to treat her grievance lightly.

———————— 84 ————————

Mrs Gaskell
1810–65

The reputation of Mrs Gaskell as a novelist has been rising in recent years – her pictures of working-class life in the North of England are more admired than used to be the case when she was thought of mainly as the biographer of Charlotte Brontë and the author of *Cranford*. She was married to a Unitarian minister in Manchester and had first-hand knowledge of the 'Two Nations' of rich and poor. In the following letter of 1854 Mrs Gaskell puts clearly before her daughter some of the practical considerations which Unitarianism involved for her, and makes the special point that it is the direct invocations of Christ in the Anglican Litany which Unitarians find impossible to accept:

I have been thinking about Church. I quite agree with you in feeling more devotional in Church than in Chapel; and I wish our Puritan ancestors had not left out so much that they might have kept in of the beautiful and impressive Church service. But I always do feel as if the Litany – the beginning of it I mean – and one or two other parts did so completely go against my belief that it would be wrong to deaden my sense of its serious error by hearing it too often. It seems to me so distinctly to go against some of the clearest of our Saviour's words in which he so expressly tells us to pray to God alone. My own wish would be that you should go to Chapel in the morning, and to Church in the evening, when there is nothing except the Doxology to offend one's sense of truth. I am sure this would be right for me; although I am so fond of the Church service and prayers as a whole that I should feel tempted as you do. With our feelings and preference for the Church service I think it is a temptation not to have a fixed belief; but I know it is wrong not to clear our minds as much as possible as to the nature of that God, and tender Saviour, whom we can not love properly unless we try and define them clearly to ourselves. Do you understand me my darling! I have often wished to talk to you about this. Then the one thing I am clear and sure about is that Jesus Christ was not equal to His Father; that, however divine a being he was not God; and that worship as God addressed to Him is therefore wrong in me; and that it is my duty to deny myself the gratification of constantly attending a service (like the morning service) in a part of which I thoroughly disagree . . .

85

John Bright
1811–89

John Bright, a Quaker from Lancashire, the son of a mill-owner, co-operated with Richard Cobden in the great effort made in the 1830s and 1840s to get the import taxes on food (the Corn Laws) repealed and so provide food that working people could afford to buy. It was a very hard struggle and he and Cobden, as two of the most notable members of the Anti-Corn Law League, faced a barrage of hostility from landowners and from members of both Houses of Parliament, who specially resented Bright's superb oratory, and the habit of the two friends of carrying their campaigning into agricultural districts where the agricultural labourers and even some farmers were influenced against the wishes of their landlords. After repeal was achieved, Bright, as an MP, continued to be active for many radical reforms, including the extension of the franchise, and used the tremendous admiration and support he had gained all over the country to further these ends. But on the outbreak of the Crimean War, which was attended by an extraordinary amount of flippant and heartless jingoism, he sacrificed his popularity without a moment's hesitation by his opposition to it – believing and feeling that it was unnecessary and wicked – and some of his greatest speeches were made to a hostile House of Commons, which realized, even when at its angriest, the incredible power and beauty of his words. For the rest of his life he occupied a unique place in Parliamentary life: his example and views carried remarkable weight with fellow MPs (his disapproval of Gladstone's later Irish policy was very influential). He represented, to a unique degree, the power and conscience of Nonconformity in a Parliament still largely upper-class and Anglican. He is buried in the Quaker cemetery in Rochdale.

He could be scathing about established religion, having fought and won battles in his youth with the Church of England's local power in Lancashire. He wrote to Villiers in 1852:

At present no Government dare say a word to the Church – that overgrown and monstrous abuse assumes airs as if it were not an abuse. It is a wen *upon the head and pretends to be the* head, *and no administration is strong enough to say a word against it. With 14,000 Dissenting Chapels in England and Wales, with two-thirds of Scotland in dissenting ranks, with five-sixths of Ireland hostile to the Church, how comes it that this scandalous abuse puts on the character of a national and useful institution? Simply because it has the Crown and the Peers on its side by tradition and the constitution, and has gained great power in the Commons thro' our defective representations. Let the representation be amended and then the Church will be more humble, and will submit, of necessity, to be overhauled as one of the departments of state.*

Lord Morley has said that the most impressive and pure piece of religion that he ever witnessed was John Bright reading a chapter of the Bible to his maid-servants, shortly after his wife's death, in his beautiful and feeling voice, followed by the Quaker silence.

86

Archbishop Tait
1811–82

English anti-clericalism goes back long before Wolsey (one only has to read the ballads of Robin Hood), but Wolsey's grandiloquence certainly seems to have provoked a feeling among the laity of 'Never again!' Lay depredations on church property in the sixteenth century were not *just* due to the greed of courtiers – one senses a real glee in cutting the clergy down to size after the way they had over-played their hand in the late Middle Ages. The feeling has remained primarily moral, social and ceremonial not, as in France, primarily intellectual or political (though MPs have retained a suspicion of clergymen – whether it be the Whig MPs of the 1830s detesting reactionary clergymen or reactionary MPs of the 1930s detesting William Temple).

But certain clergy, in every generation, have managed to diminish, not increase, anti-clericalism. One of the greatest was Archibald Campbell Tait, the first Scottish Archbishop of Canterbury from 1869 to 1882. When he became Bishop of London he immediately set to work on his two great aims – to make the Church of England the church of the poor and of the nation as a whole. He was a man whose sympathies had been enlarged, not narrowed, by suffering: he had poor health himself and he and his wife had endured the appalling tragedy of losing five small children of scarlet fever in the course of one month. He caused a good deal of scandal amongst conventional friends by his insistence on evangelistic work, going so far as to preach in the open air to gypsies, 'Behaving like a Methodist!' His life, written by Randall Davidson, shows that if a man is great enough he can be a hero both to his chaplain and his son-in-law.

From Tait's prayer on being appointed Bishop of London:

O Lord! grant that Thy Church may take no injury through my fault. Give me vigilance over myself first, next over others. Enable me to arrange my days and all my time so as to have ample time for prayer and study of Thy word. Give me wisdom – give me holiness – give me strength of mind and body – give me kind consideration for the feelings of all around me – give me boldness – give me decision.

──────────── 87 ────────────

Dean Church
1815–90

Richard William Church became the friend and follower of Newman while at Oxford, but when Newman was converted to Roman Catholicism in 1845, Church remained an Anglican. He wrote and preached throughout a long life, first as a country parson but later as Dean of St Paul's, stressing continually the duty of everyone to do the best they possibly could for the service of God, without fretting too much as to what might happen in the future or whether their work might be superseded. He was a most important link between the worlds of religion and science, and between Anglicans of very different views; he wrote widely, often in the church weekly *The Guardian*, of which he was a founder. He was a frequent correspondence of Gladstone's on church matters.

He wrote to a friend about the perplexities of pain in the world and the ambiguities in life:

Here are facts and phenomena on both sides, some leading to belief, some to unbelief; and we human creatures, with our affections, our hopes and wishes and our wills, stand, as it were, solicited by either set of facts. The facts which witness to the goodness and the love of God are clear and undeniable; they are not got rid of by the presence and certainty of other facts, which seem of an opposite kind; only the co-existence of the two contraries is perplexing. And then comes the question, which shall have the governing influence on wills and lives? You must, by the necessity of your existence, trust one set of appearances; which will you trust? Our Lord came among us not to clear up the perplexity, but to show us which side to take.

He preached a very severe sermon on 'The Imperfections of Religious Men':

The challenge, as he saw it, consisted not in the story of personal weaknesses such as are common to men, but the shortcomings and failures peculiar to religious persons and 'the faults of their religion itself'. If anyone thinks, says the preacher, that God when He sent the light of His truth into the world would safeguard it from the possibility of being corrupted by His servants, he need only read the Bible to be undeceived. 'His first and primary gift to man is that he is a free moral agent: and with that He has given nothing to man . . . which man may not, if he will, abuse and spoil.' The recorded behaviour of the custodians of the Gospel, from the very days of the Apostles and since, should instruct us what to expect. The zeal and vehemence of great teachers and champions of the faith in the fight against heresy were not infrequently the means of letting loose a spirit quite alien to that of Christ's love. 'There is scarcely a true principle of religious faith, there is scarcely a natural and pure instinct of worship, there is scarcely a noble work of self-devotion and usefulness, there is scarcely a wisely planned and generous institution, on which the mistakes of good men have not brought discredit, perhaps at last extinguished and abolished it.' Arising out of such considerations a further conclusion can hardly be escaped. The imperfections of the Christian Church itself at every period must not be blinked. 'The ideal of sanctity, of infallibility, of consistency, of unity, is what ought to have been; what has been, is matter of history.'

88

Benjamin Jowett
1817–93

The fame of the Tutor and Master of Balliol has tended to over-shadow Jowett's courageous work to break the silence, which covered Oxford in his early years there, on everything connected with biblical criticism. He was first suspected for liberalism in religion in the 1850s, when he criticized the extreme legal theory of the atonement in his commentary on St Paul, and then the publication of *Essays and Reviews* in 1860 brought much trouble on him and for years he suffered because of his desire to bring truth and reality into the *Interpretation of Scripture*, which was the title of his contribution to that book. Later in life he achieved an immense work of teaching and pastoral supervision for Balliol, raising its whole position in English life and at the same time writing his great work on Plato, but it is his courage and dignity in the years of struggle which entitle him to the greatest admiration.

From a letter to Benjamin Brodie, afterwards Professor of Chemistry, written in 1844:

What appears to me to make the greatest gulph between us is not your taking a rationalistic or mythic view of the Bible, or difficulties about miracles, or even prayer, but that you do not leave any place for religion at all, so that although you may hold the being of God as the Author of the Universe, I do not see how you would be worse off morally if Atheism were proved to demonstration. What would you lose but a little poetry which is a very weak motive to holiness of Life? And having shut yourself out from any moral relation to God as an incentive to Duty does this moral Atheism satisfy human nature?

Sir Henry Acland, Jowett's physician, recalled how:

One night when Jowett heard I was sleepless, he came quietly into my room, sat by the bedside, and said in that small voice once heard never to be forgotten, 'You are very unwell. I will read to you'; and he read in the same voice the 14th chapter of St John and said 'I hope you will feel better', and went away. I often, often have thought (of) this during Oxford Controversies.

In 1846 he wrote to Stanley (later Dean of Westminster) who shared many of his views:

Considering how little sympathy I have with the clergy, for I never hear a sermon scarcely which does not seem equally divided between truth and falsehood, it seems like a kind of treachery to be one of them. But I really believe that treachery to the clergy is loyalty to the Church, and that if religion is to be saved at all it must be through the laity and statesmen, etc., not through the clergy.

In 1855, in his essay *On Atonement and Satisfaction* he wrote:

God is represented as angry with us for what we never did; He is ready to inflict a disproportionate punishment on us for what we are; He is satisfied by the sufferings of His Son in our stead . . . The imperfection of human law is transferred to the Divine . . . The death of Christ is also explained by the analogy of the ancient rite of sacrifice. He is a victim laid upon the altar to appease the wrath of God . . . I shall endeavour to show, 1, that these conceptions of the work of Christ have no foundation in Scripture; 2, that their growth may be traced in ecclesiastical history; 3, that the only sacrifice, atonement, or satisfaction, with which the Christian has to do, is a moral and spiritual one; not the pouring out of blood upon the earth; but the living sacrifice 'to do thy will, O God'; in which the believer has part as well as his Lord; about the meaning of which there can be no more question in our day than there was in the first ages.

Archbishop Lang wrote:

Jowett, I remember, had said in one of his quaint and characteristic Balliol Sermons, 'The search for truth is one thing; fluttering after it is another.'

89

Prince Albert
1819–61

It is sad to read of the spirited young man whom Queen Victoria married turning so quickly into the tired, serious and grossly overworked Prince Consort who died at only forty-two. He realized – it was brutally emphasized during the Crimean War when a number of baseless scandals were circulated about him – that he was never popular in England. He was too serious, too formal, too pernickety for most of his English contemporaries. He found his escape in working harder and harder and much of what he did has been of lasting benefit to his adopted country. But there seems to have been something more than discouragement, some streak of melancholy or lack of vitality, which became more noticeable in the last years of his life. He drove himself with German conscientiousness, but he paid a very heavy price for it.

This letter was written in 1845 when Samuel Wilberforce, a favourite preacher at Court, was appointed Bishop of Oxford. The Prince was then in his mid-twenties!

Windsor Castle, 19th October, 1845.

My dear Dean, I had intended to commit to paper for you my views on the position of a Bishop in the House of Lords, but gave up the idea, fearing that it might appear presumptuous on my part. Anson, however, tells me that he is sure you would not consider it as such, and would be pleased if I were still to do it; I accordingly resume the pen.

A Bishop ought to abstain completely *from mixing himself up with the politics of the day, and beyond giving a general support to the* Queen's Government, *and occasionally voting for it, should take no part in the discussions of State affairs (for instance, Corn Laws, Game Laws, Trade or Financial questions, &c., &c.,); but he should come forward whenever the interests of Humanity are at stake, and give boldly and manfully his advice to the House and Country (I mean questions like Negro Emancipation, education of the people, improvement of the health of towns, measures for the recreation of the poor, against cruelty to animals, for regulating factory labour, &c., &c.,).*

As to religious affairs, he cannot but take an active part in them; but let that always be the part of a Christian, *not of a mere* Churchman. *Let him never forget the insufficiency of human knowledge and wisdom, and the impossibility for any man, or even Church, to say, 'I am right, and I alone am right.' Let him, therefore, be meek, and liberal, and tolerant to other confessions; but let him never forget that he is a representative of the Church of the Land, the maintenance of which is as important to the country as that of its Constitution or its Throne. Let him, here, always be conscious that the Church has duties to fulfil, that it does not exist for itself, but for the people, for the country, and that it ought to have no higher aim than to be the Church of the people. Let there be, therefore, no calling for new rights, privileges, grants, &c., but show the zeal and capacity of the Church to stretch her powers and capabilities to the utmost for the fulfilment of her sacred duties to the people, in ministering and teaching. A Bishop ought to be uniformly a peace-maker, and, when he can, it is his duty to lessen political and other animosities, and remind the Peers of their duties as Christians. He ought to be a guardian of public morality, not, like the press, by tediously interfering with every man's private affairs,*

speaking for applause, or trampling on those that are fallen, but by
watching over the morality of the State in acts which expediency or hope for
profit may tempt it to commit, as well in home and colonial as in foreign
affairs.

He should likewise boldly admonish the public even against its
predominant feeling, if this be contrary to the purest standard of morality
(reproving, for instance, the recklessness and the wickedness of the
Projectors of Railway schemes, who, having no funds themselves, acquire
riches at the expense of others, their dupes). Here the nation is in the
greatest danger, as every individual gets corrupted, and every sense of
shame is lost.

In this way the Bishops would become a powerful force in the Lords, and
the country would feel that their presence there supplies a great want, and
is a great protection to the people.

I have spoken as thoughts have struck me, and am sure you will be better
able than I am to take a comprehensive view of the position. Ever yours
truly, ALBERT.

90

Queen Victoria
1819–1901

None of the characteristic forms of *English* Victorian piety
really seem to have suited the Queen herself – she was
happiest with the Church of Scotland, which she attended
when at Balmoral. She felt that frequent communions could
become irreverent: she said that three months was not too
much time to give to preparation. Probably she was
influenced in religious preferences by the Prince Consort's
Lutheranism, as she was in so many matters of conduct. (Her
court was very different in atmosphere from that of her uncles
and predecessors and her example had a widespread effect.)
She was exceedingly shrewd over Church of England
appointments – always preferring 'Broad Churchmen' to
either High Church or extreme Evangelical candidates – and
she exerted considerable influence on all her Prime Ministers
in these affairs. Certain English churchmen did manage to
please her because of their combination of common sense and

warmth of heart, Randall Davidson, Dean of Windsor, being the most notable of these.

The following letter shows the Queen's tolerance: there had been a great political fuss because the Pope had given English territorial titles to some of his bishops. Queen Victoria wrote about it to her aunt, the Duchess of Gloucester, on 12 December 1850:

> I am glad that you are pleased with my answers to the Addresses; I thought them very proper.
>
> I would never have consented to say anything which breathed a spirit of intolerance. Sincerely Protestant as I always have been and always shall be, and indignant as I am at those who call themselves Protestants, while they in fact are quite the contrary, I much regret the unchristian and intolerant spirit exhibited by many people at public meetings. I cannot bear to hear the violent abuse of the Catholic religion, which is so painful and cruel towards the many good and innocent Roman Catholics. However, we must hope and trust this excitement will soon cease, and that the wholesome effect of it on our own Church will be the lasting result of it. Ever yours . . .

The Queen doubtless thought that the effect of the agitation might be to quell the extreme High Churchmen in the Church of England.

She expressed herself briskly about prayers against the cholera, which was terrifying people in the 1850s much as AIDS does today, in a letter to her Prime Minister, Lord Aberdeen, in August 1854:

> The Queen must repeat what she has frequently done, that she strongly objects to these special prayers which are, in fact, not a sign of gratitude or confidence in the Almighty – for if this is the course to be pursued, we ought to have one for every illness, and certainly in '37 the influenza was notoriously more fatal than the cholera had ever been, and yet no one would have thought of having a prayer against that. Our Liturgy has provided for these calamities, and we may have frequent returns of the cholera – and yet it would be difficult to define the number of deaths which are to make 'a form of prayer' necessary. The Queen would, therefore, strongly recommend the usual prayer being used, and no other, as is the case for prayer in time of War. What is the use of the prayers in the Liturgy, which were no doubt composed when we were subject to other equally fatal diseases, if a new one is always to be framed specially for the cholera?

The Queen would wish Lord Aberdeen to give this as her decided opinion to the Archbishop, at all events for the present. Last year the cholera quite decimated Newcastle, and was bad in many other places, but there was no special prayer, and now the illness is in London but not in any other place, a prayer is proposed by the Archbishop. The Queen cannot see the difference between the one and the other.

91

Archbishop Frederick Temple
1821–1902

Frederick Temple became a liberal in theology at Oxford, where he had many academic successes, in spite of being so poor that he is said to have studied by the passage light at night, to save candles. His participation in the famous *Essays and Reviews* of 1860, which first really brought the whole matter of biblical criticism to public notice in England, caused trouble during his headmastership of Rugby and nearly prevented his consecration as Bishop of Exeter. But he succeeded in both places – he was the headmaster of whom a boy wrote: 'A beast, but a just beast,' and also the only one known to have climbed all the elm trees in the School Close. He became an outstanding bishop and was later translated to London and then to Canterbury. He was described, when preaching, as 'granite on fire'. As an old man he crowned Edward VII.

Temple had refused to go into explanations of *Essays and Reviews* before he became a bishop, but in 1870 he spoke out in Convocation:

It seems to me that, whether we like it or not, we are of necessity involved in what Dr Arnold spoke of some years ago – namely, the general discussion, all over the Christian world, of the degree and limits of the inspiration of the Bible. It is a question of absolutely enormous importance. The progress of discovery and historical research has made it quite impossible for us to leave it alone; it is forced upon us on every side. It is quite impossible that this great discussion should really come to a worthy end unless it is conducted with real freedom on the part of those who take any real share in it . . . . I think that such a discussion ought to be allowed the greatest freedom that can possibly be given it, consistent with the acknowledgment of the Bible as the supreme revelation and with a reverent – a really reverent – spirit in the treatment of all subjects connected with it.

In a letter of 1898 to his son William, then aged seventeen:

I who have read the Bible regularly for nearly seventy years always feel that if my conscience differs from the Bible I must pause. It may be my conscience wants enlightenment. It may be that I do not rightly interpret the Bible. But I do not feel the same with any other book.

— 92 —

Charlotte Mary Yonge
1823–1901

One of the most prolific novelists of the nineteenth century, Charlotte Yonge is chiefly remembered for her most famous book *The Heir of Redclyffe*, published in 1853 and an immediate bestseller. But, as the neighbour and pupil of John Keble, much of what she wrote throws floods of light upon the church movement begun in Oxford in the 1830s, which in her maturity was working itself out in the parishes of England. A novel such as her *Pillars of the House* vividly presents what the Tractarian clergy were trying to achieve.

As well as writing novels and historical works she edited periodicals for girls, wrote on the Bible for children and produced essays. She never married, but remained in Otterbourne, near Winchester, all her life.

From a book of essays, *Womankind*, of 1876:

[Churchgoing] ought to be looked on as our regular homage to God, and therefore to be made the first consideration in all our arrangements, never to be sacrificed for any consideration short of illness or absolute duty . . . the forcing ourselves to put our duty to God above all else, is the way to learn the love of God . . . Going to Church is not only, nor chiefly, to do ourselves good. It is primarily to praise God.

Writing of sorrow in the same book:

The Christian no longer feels as if 'some strange thing happened to him,' but remembers that the Saviour's prayer, 'Not My will, but Thine be done,' has been handed on to him. He knows that his Master does not feel for him mere external pity, but the actual sympathy of a fellow sufferer.

Yes, it is easy to talk till the trial comes, and the agonized heart feels as if it were all a failure and a hollowness, and those things were utterly powerless as a comfort. . . . It is only the religion that is already a part of our lives that gives us real strength and comfort in trouble.

93

Bishop Westcott
1825–1901

One of the greatest New Testament scholars of any age, Brooke Foss Westcott was Regius Professor of Divinity at Cambridge from 1870 to 1890 and later Bishop of Durham. He took part in the translation of the Revised Version of the Bible, but perhaps his greatest academic achievement was the critical Greek text of the New Testament, published in 1881, on which he had worked for many years with his friend F. J. A. Hort. Westcott was eager for the best possible training for the clergy, and the training college Westcott House at Cambridge is called after him. He was a much loved Bishop of Durham and did a great work of conciliation between the different sides in industry; he was regarded as a champion of the miners. His own tastes and ways were very simple; he found his relaxation in sketching and botany and his delight was immense when his children clubbed together to buy him a tricycle!

A prayer which he constantly used:

Blessed Lord, by Whose Providence all Holy Scriptures were written and preserved for our instruction, give us grace to study them each day with patience and love. Strengthen our souls with the fulness of Thy divine teaching. Keep from us all pride and irreverence. Guide us in the deep things of Thy heavenly wisdom; and, of Thy great mercy, lead us by Thy Word into everlasting life, through Jesus Christ our Saviour. Amen.

Josephine Butler
1828–1906

Josephine Butler was subjected to misrepresentation, insults, threats and actual physical violence for her championship of prostitutes and her determination to get the worst of the laws against them repealed. It is difficult to realize the immense number of women in Victorian England driven into prostitution by sheer economic pressure: also the extent to which it was a forbidden topic for 'virtuous' women. Mrs Butler broke through this silence and also took homeless, sick and dying women into her own home to care for them. She was supported in her struggle by a very happy marriage and by a group of devoted friends, but it took from 1869 to 1886 to get the 'Contagious Diseases Act' repealed, and after that she was still active for the cause in other countries and especially against the exploitation of children.

In 1886 she warned a great meeting at Exeter Hall that they must not trust too much in organization:

Someone has lately spoken of the Apostolic order in the evolution of a great reform. First He gave them apostles and prophets; afterwards teachers and evangelists. Let us be sure that we are not in any of our national sections working fruitlessly in a reverse order; beginning, so to speak, at the wrong end; over-estimating the utility of machinery; and forgetting a little the essential thing, the power of the unseen Spirit, which bloweth where it listeth; like the wind of heaven, which you cannot bind or drill or regulate . . . Seek men and women first – before any machinery. If you have not got them, seek the breath of that wind which will breathe upon the dry bones and make them live and spring to their feet . . . When the era of teachers and evangelists arrives, then organization becomes a necessity. Order, the law of God's universe, must be applied. But do, dear friends, beware of thinking that organization is the first and most important thing. Beware of thinking that good statutes, rules, a sound financial basis, a regular income are needful, before you can make any effectual attack on an enemy which is daily and hourly – at this very hour – murdering souls and bodies.

Our Father in heaven knows that we have need of material resources; and He will justify the faith that steps boldly forth, before all these things are seen visibly to exist.

Robert William Dale
1829–95

Of all the great Freechurchmen of the nineteenth century, Robert Dale must have been the most versatile. He was minister for many years of the Congregational Chapel of Carr's Lane in Birmingham, he took part in many schemes for the improvement of Birmingham, he wrote, preached and lectured, compiled the *English Hymn Book* published in 1874, and he was the confidant and adviser of many people in public life, including Joseph Chamberlain. His teaching had two great themes: that the love of God was shown at its height in the resurrection and that our love of God must be witnessed to by our care for others. His work was greatly appreciated by men of other denominations, but he remained a fervent Congregationalist in every way. His comments on other churches could be acute and searching and he was deeply involved in the nineteenth century's disputes over the different churches' role in education. He was constantly aware of what Congregationalism could and should be giving to the life of the people of England and of the splendours of its traditions and history.

From a sermon of the 1850s:

In these days when it is a universal lamentation that many of our most vigorous minds are quite uncontrolled and even uninterested by Christian teaching, and when the increasing disregard of the peculiar doctrines of the New Testament is perpetually acknowledged and loudly deplored, it cannot be the duty of the Christian minister to drive away from the church all the thoughtful people that are left, by adopting a style of preaching that calls for no intellectual activity, or to confirm and sanction the general depreciation of the importance of Christian doctrines, by avoiding the discussions through which alone these doctrines can be established. As a Christian congregation it should be as much our ambition to be as much distinguished for breadth and depth of religious knowledge as for fervour of devotion, freedom of generosity and nobleness of moral character; and there is a more intimate connection than some of us, perhaps, are inclined to believe, between spiritual truth in the intellect and spiritual life in the heart. I think that God could hardly confer upon this country a greater blessing than by re-awakening that intense interest in religious doctrine which distinguished the heroic men who belonged to the times of the Commonwealth.

Dale's biographer describes:

Dale was spending a summer holiday in Grasmere, and had walked over to Patterdale to spend the day with Dr Abbott, the headmaster of the City of London School, an able and prominent Broad Churchman (Anglican). In the early evening this friend started with him to set him on his way home, still intent on the questions, religious and ecclesiastical, which they had discussed for many hours.

We were walking together from the head of Ullswater up towards the foot of Grisdale Tarn, and he asked me, with an expression of astonishment and incredulity, whether I really thought that if the shepherds of Patterdale – a dozen or score of them – determined to constitute themselves a Congregational Church, it was possible for such a church to fulfil the purposes for which churches exist. To such a question there could be but one answer. Great natural sagacity, high intellectual culture, however admirable, are not essential: 'It is enough if, when they meet, they really meet in Christ's name – but no man can say that Jesus is Lord but by the Holy Ghost.'

Archbishop Benson
1829–96

Edward White Benson, an Anglican, was the originator of the famous service of nine lessons and carols, now widely used at Christmas time, and this is an appropriate memorial to him as he was deeply interested in history, in tradition and in the services of the church. (But he was far from blindly devoted to the church; as early as 1870 he wrote to his wife saying he felt it was vital to teach children 'that it is a Society – not an ideal person – to talk of it as "it", not as "she" – to obey its laws with a sense that they are like other laws – and to feel that there is no absolute trust to be placed anywhere but in Him in whom Humanity and Divinity are summed up. Those two elements of Life Everlasting are *not* united in the Church. We have to *improve* the Church, and to place our faith only in the Head.')

The two quotations that follow illustrate what many other subsequent archbishops must have felt: the fearful strain that the office of archbishop places on the holder. Benson had fourteen years of it, from 1882 to 1896, and there were many disputes and stresses in the Church of England at that time and the reputation and influence of the office was constantly growing, as well overseas as at home.

June 16 1884, from Benson's journal:

The first year of my Archiepiscopate, when everything within and without, crowded business, details, talk, grind, meetings, interviews, letters, without stop or stay, from early to past midnight; I thought I would acquiesce in it as God's will and trust Him to feed me spiritually in the midst of this current. But He did not, and will not, and I thank Him. Little as I have lately got of separate moments, it is a great blessing, and it is clear that to get it is one's true work – and to refuse false work.

October 10, 1884, from Benson's journal:

How can one help perplexing oneself in such a place as this? I find in myself no fitness for it. I could not resist, I had no right to resist. If calls exist, called I was; against my will. An unfit man, not unfit in his humility subjective, but clearly seeing himself by God's help as he is – yet called. Follows from that, that there is something unknown in God's counsels for the Church and for His poor servant, whom he will not let fall to the ground for simply nothing, for His own love to the least – something he means to have done by one unfit for the great place. Well then, he will be fit for the thing He wants to have done. Then make him fit – and let, O God, whatever it be, be good for Thy Church. It is in Thy hand.

97

Dorothea Beale
1831–1906

The headmistress of Cheltenham Ladies' College from 1858 to her death was a woman of great spiritual depth: it is recorded that she found in the doctrine of the resurrection her great strength and hope. Some of the girls once brought her a water-lily stem with a dragonfly clinging to it, just emerging from its chrysalis, and she often used this as a symbol of what she believed. In the middle of her life she suffered an agonizing trial: she thought she was losing her faith, but she emerged from her suffering and her work was again based on her belief in God's demands and God's guidance. She was active in many sides of women's education, including the founding of the first English training college for secondary school women teachers and of St Hilda's College, Oxford. She was a close friend of Miss Buss, the great London headmistress and founder of the North London Collegiate School. Often, when they met, they would repeat together the *Veni Creator Spiritus*.

In her opening address to the Teachers' College Miss Beale said:

There is only one motive power which can sustain the worker, and especially the teacher, and that is faith in God . . . The only thing to make us teach with joy and energy . . . is the thought which moved the Apostle of old, that our labour is not in vain in the Lord.

The life of the teacher, she asserted, is to be,

not a pleasant but a noble life (and that must be a blessed life), a life of earnest effort.

'I shall never forget the impression I received as quite a young girl,' wrote one of her pupils 'when I heard her read the first chapter of St John's Gospel. It was quite electric, one felt that this woman was reading the thing she considered the greatest in the world.'

———————— 98 ————————

Octavia Hill
1838–1912

The great pioneer of better accommodation for poor people in London began her work with a few houses in 1865: from the first she insisted that only by knowing and respecting the tenants personally could any lasting success be achieved. Her work expanded, she taught her methods to others, and she became an authority on the management of property. This led her to concern herself with safeguarding open spaces and so to become one of the founders of the National Trust. Her mother, a remarkable woman, had given her a secure and happy childhood but little explicit religious teaching. In her teens Octavia came under the influence of F. D. Maurice, the great exponent of Christian concern for bodies as well as souls, and through him she became an Anglican:

It was Mr Maurice who showed me a life in the Creeds, the services and the Bible; who interpreted for me much that was dark and puzzling in life; how the belief in a Father, Son and Holy Ghost might be a most real faith, not a dead notion, that I might believe not only that God was manifesting Himself to each man in the inward consciousness of light and beauty . . . but that a Real Person had come among us, whose will had been brought into harmony with His . . . that He had declared that we might have Life, that Life was knowledge of God.

Lady Frederick Cavendish
1841–1925

Lucy Lyttelton, Mrs Gladstone's niece, married the younger son of the Duke of Devonshire who was a Liberal MP and a close follower of Gladstone. After eighteen years of happy marriage he was murdered by terrorists in Phoenix Park, Dublin, as he attempted to defend their victim, an Irish civil servant. Lord Frederick had gone to Dublin that same day to try to implement a more conciliatory policy towards Ireland. His death caused a shock similar to that of Earl Mountbatten's murder in our own time. Lucy Cavendish was one of the most golden characters imaginable: a supporter of every good cause, entirely unspoilt by her position and greatly beloved. Only her piety – the most extensive Anglican observance – sometimes troubled the less devout. 'Church is Lucy's public house,' said a friend, 'and the worst of it is, there's no keeping her out of it.' Her diaries are a valuable source for Victorian history and display the Lyttelton family's passionate interest in church matters. (Lucy Cavendish College, Cambridge, is called after her, as a tribute to her work for education.)

December 19th, 1966. Dr Pusey is waging a war in The Times *upon Private Confession and Absolution, which he advocates most strongly, tho' not condemning those who differ from him. It seems to me quite wrong to oppose private confession if it is quite voluntary; but it is all but inconceivable to me. Many things it would be entirely impossible to put into spoken words, and so one would be false; then under or over-statement of others would be inevitable; as to motives, one would get into hopeless perplexity; and then there is forgetfulness. My strong feeling (and I know it is not pride) is 'O keep the softening veil in mercy drawn,* Thou who canst love us, though Thou read us true;' *and no special confession to man, that I can imagine, could be to me what the silent appeal of one's soul is, lying with tears at His feet Who sees all, and pities all. 'O Lord,* Thou knowest.' *Then comes the message of the priest, as if straight from Heaven*

– more consoling and reuniting, to my mind, than if the preceding confession had been a set one to him.

About her reaction to her husband's murder, her sister, Mrs Talbot, wrote:

To be with Lucy through those first hours of her great sorrow was to be allowed to see a marvellous manifestation of the power of religion, and of the blessedness granted to those who all their lives have kept their faith in God pure and strong. Her faith never failed her for one instant; it was there, ready to her hand. She had not to look for it, but only to lean heavily upon it, and she was enabled to be patient and trustful, and absolutely without one thought of bitterness, much less of revenge on those who had shattered her earthly happiness.

———————— 100 ————————

Bishop Mandell Creighton
1843–1901

The great historian of the mediaeval papacy was also a zealous Church of England parish priest. (He was rebuked by the Roman Catholic historian, Lord Acton, for being too lenient to various wicked Popes: his reply was that it was wrong to judge people by standards of other ages than their own.) Creighton went on to be one of the most notable bishops London has had, but was felt to have worn himself out dealing with that most intractable diocese. His *Life*, by his wife, revealed many sides of a very complex personality. His terse statements could be alarming to weaker brethren: 'No people do so much harm as those who go about doing good' – but again and again there are records of his tolerance, his charity and his patience. Also of his cheerfulness: 'In dealing with ourselves after we have "let the ape and tiger die", we have to deal with the donkey, which is a more intractable and enduring animal than the others.'

From a letter to a friend written in 1886:

The Christian in proportion as he lays hold of God cannot believe in himself. Now the highest point of the Christian character is that in which we attain forgetfulness of self and act simply as God's creatures. Such is the temper seen in St Paul and St John very clearly. But this self-forgetfulness is the fruit of a long process of training in trust in God. To you and me the pain of life lies in the perpetual contrast between the aspiration of our spirit and the poor realization of our actual life. It is no wonder that people have tried at many times to simplify the problem – that they have sought a special form of life in which they might be free from ordinary temptations, the monastery, the brotherhood, the ascetic practice; but all in vain, for the difficulty lay not without, but within – not in the world, but in their own heart. The means of self-discipline lie round every path; the temptations to self-seeking beset every career: no life is itself more spiritual than any other.

To a friend, written in 1897:

So long as one bears one's own life in one's hands, the burden grows intolerable. It is only by seeing that life as part of a universal life that peace is found. And the life of man is set forth in the Life of Jesus, who gives His Spirit and His Life to those who seek it. He gives little by little as we are able to receive. We must make room for Him: all lies in that. We do not so much want opinions about life – there are plenty of them – but an object and a motive. If once you grasp this truth, the answer comes of itself. It is not we who find out God: He finds us out.

Bishop Talbot
1844–1934

The Victorians had extraordinary courage in appointing young men to great positions – never shown better than by making Edward Stuart Talbot Warden of the newly founded Keble College at Oxford at the age of twenty-five. He did a great work there, moving on to the huge parish of Leeds, and then to various bishoprics, the final one being Winchester. Talbot married Lavinia Lyttelton, Gladstone's niece, and all his life moved easily in the world of high politics, being in himself a valuable link between church and state. He was a friend of Gore and Scott Holland and one of the writers of *Lux Mundi*, a famous book published by a group of friends in 1889 which was aimed at reconciling faith and the recent discoveries in historical and biblical criticism. Talbot's life was an example of someone trying to find the will of God and then going out and doing it: he was not a mystic, or a famous spiritual guide, but he was deeply honest and sincere and ready to admit his own difficulties in order to help other people.

From a letter to Lady Welby in 1891:

Death to me is terrible, and especially for its gauntness. I shrink unspeakably from the unknown. So the great astronomical discoveries are to me, naturally, simply appalling. They make me miserably uncomfortable. To try and dwell on them would, I think, almost literally make me sick. They turn my head. So with thought. There seems to me to be a sort of ocean of tumbling ideas into which convictions and faith easily crumble. I cannot say how it appals me.

The sense of having that treasure (of Faith) seems to me to have been the abiding secret of the Church of Christ, the thing which could be shared by all, the gospel of the poor . . . The whole drift of the present day criticism is towards the conclusion that this was 'illusion' . . . It was 'a phase of thought' – 'a combination of historical forces' etc. When the consciousness of all this sweeps over me, it saddens and oppresses me. It does not find (here is my definite and specific accusation) the answer of a sure faith, a knowledge of Christ as a Living Presence as it does in Christians as open-minded as myself and more so; it gives me the shivers. But I should be false, cowardly, ungrateful, if I did not recognize another side. The sense of 'gauntness', etc., is (I have realized with thanks) the touch of that awefulness of God which has always been a side of true religion. We ought not to think that we hold Him. And so it has become more real to me to feel that my faith is His gift and not my achievement – that I am known of Him rather than that I know Him. And in this sense I am brought to something more like a primitive and permanent Christian temper. Only its sureness! Well, the want of that is discipline, is chastisement. And perhaps He may give more of it in His own time.

In view of the foregoing, it is good to know that when Bishop Talbot did die, at a great age, it was peacefully, easily, and, as far as anyone can know, happily.

The Earl of Rosebery
1847–1929

The man who succeeded Mr Gladstone as Prime Minister in 1894 was as different from his predecessor as it was possible to be – except that they were both Liberals, Scotsmen and highly educated. Rosebery was in favour of what was then called 'Imperialism', exceedingly sensitive, even touchy, without the power to dominate a strong-minded Cabinet and without that overmastering passion for politics which sustains people in ministerial life. He resigned the leadership of the Liberal party in 1896 on what seems to have been very insufficient grounds, and never resumed it, but remained like some mysterious oracle liable to emerge from seclusion with brilliant pronouncements on a surprising variety of matters. Reading the various biographies it appears likely that he never recovered from the death in 1890 of his wife, Hannah de Rothschild; the marriage had been a very happy one: she had kept her Jewish faith and he his Christianity.

The following is part of a letter which he wrote after Lady Rosebery's death to his friend Henry Scott Holland:

I pass through the valley of the shadow of death. And in that valley are all the stations of the cross by which one cannot but pause and meditate, whether one will or no: the great problems of life and eternity suddenly gape open on each side and will not be denied: they have each to be contemplated or considered. And so one is led to believe that Death, besides what it means for the one taken, is for the one or for those surviving the supreme warning of God, the call of the trumpet second only to the last; the summons to face once and for all the awe and import of the visible and invisible world. And so one is led by the grim angel through a pilgrimage like that in the cartoons of Faust, where all that is actual or possible or past is lit up by the flashes of his lantern, and the blessed dead wrapped in real rest – a distant star of comfort.

John Richardson Illingworth
1848–1915

Because of poor health John Illingworth was unable to continue with his university career (he had spent some years in Oxford teaching at the newly founded Keble College). He became rector of Longworth, a country parish in Berkshire and remained there for the rest of his life. While there he kept in touch with a group of his friends, including Charles Gore, Henry Scott Holland and Edward Talbot, who joined together to publish the important book *Lux Mundi* in 1889. They were accustomed to meet at Longworth every year and they gave the east window to the church to commemorate their co-operation and friendship.

The following letter describes what Illingworth felt should be undertaken by a friend, but it also in fact describes the aim of *Lux Mundi*.

You are familiar enough with the thought that Christian truth, in virtue of its very vitality, is and must be for ever outgrowing the clothes with which successive ages invest it . . . and I think if you will keep the distinction in mind between the truth *and its* expression *– the* spirit *and the* letter*, it will help you. For we are living at one of those epochs when a resetting of the Truth, a restatement of it in more adequate language, has become imperatively necessary. All round us men are thirsting for such a restatement, and many and many are rejecting Christianity simply because it has never been put before them in the form which their reason and their conscience alike demand. And every man who feels this inadequacy of the current theological statements, like yourself, much more every ordained teacher of others, as the clergy are, is, as you justly say, under a very great and serious responsibility before God to assist in the purification of the temple of theology. The change that has to be made is like the change of the services at the Reformation, from the Latin to the Vernacular. Nor need you think it presumptuous to suppose such a change necessary. The theology of the past gains a fictitious unity for us, chiefly from our* *ignorance of it. The more we look into it, the more we find that it has changed its language again and again – and changed it under the guidance of that only kind of Vox populi which can be truly called Vox Dei – i.e. the gradually swelling murmur of thoughtful and earnest men, both within and without the Christian pale, claiming to correct the current teaching, because their hearts and consciences felt it to be unworthy.*

--------------------- 104 ---------------------

Archbishop Davidson
1848–1930

Frederick and William Temple are the only father and son both to be Archbishops of Canterbury, and Archbishop Tait and Archbishop Davidson are the only father-in-law and son-in-law who both held that office. Randall Davidson was chaplain to Tait, and helped him greatly in his later years, learning from him the belief in the Church of England as a national church – the church of all the people; and also to regard seriously the duty of Canterbury to help and advise (though not to attempt to control) the Anglican churches overseas. Davidson became Archbishop in 1903 and resigned in 1928, and during those twenty-five years he worked incessantly for harmony and consensus, both in the church and nation. His *Life*, by Bishop Bell of Chichester, is one of the great biographies of all time, and displays his endless patience and tact: showing how appeals from every side flooded into Lambeth and how unstintingly he worked to help all who called on him. He was accustomed to pray: 'Grant O Lord, that in the weariness of unceasing work our intercourse with thee may ever be fresh.' Some critics thought that he was too 'establishment', too inclined to consider what the House of Lords might think, but the answer his biographer implies is that in the terrible years of the First World War and its aftermath the Church of England needed a steady hand and a quiet voice, and that is what God provided. The Archbishop was greatly esteemed by Free-churchmen, and it was while he was at Lambeth that the first great hopes for reunion were voiced in the 'Appeal to all Christian People' of 1920, made by the Anglican bishops.

The Archbishop once gave a sermon on 'Prayer and Business' and his biographer comments that what Davidson said about the prophet Daniel revealed a great deal about the preacher's own behaviour:

The story of Daniel sets before us no picture of a mystic visionary, an ascetic thinker living outside the stream and swing of the world's life. He is set before us as a busy man of affairs, with a huge trust laid upon him for active administrative service; immersed, as we should nowadays express it, in public business. But on the life is set the stamp of faithfulness to God, whatever that faithfulness might cost . . . This man, of quiet, unflinching, prayerful purpose, avowedly took the work which was allotted to him — the public work in a heathen capital — as of Divine appointing, to be done to the very best of his power under the all-seeing eye and the personal guidance of the Lord his God . . . But the two sides or divisions of his life were inseparably one . . . The vividness of his communion with God is not one whit restrained or marred by his secular work, nor must that secular work — those prosaic, responsible duties of his office and calling — be set aside or disregarded even when there has come to him the deepest, the most overwhelming of spiritual visions or messages from on high.

105

Bishop Paget
1851–1911

Most of Bishop Paget's life was spent in Oxford, the happiest part, perhaps, when Dean of Christchurch. He was married to a daughter of Dean Church of St Paul's, and learnt much from his father-in-law. He was one of the group of contributors to *Lux Mundi*, published in 1889 – he wrote on the sacraments. His wife died in 1900, before he became Bishop of Oxford, and he had to struggle through his episcopacy without her. He laid particular stress, in his teaching, on strict truthfulness.

From a letter written to a friend, asking him to be godfather to his eldest child:

. . . we are anxious that among the chief and nearest influences on our boy's life there should be the example and advice of those who will give him

wider views of life than are apt to be given by the daily talk and interest of a parish priest's home: we want him to see from the first how much bigger a thing Christianity is than that clerical aspect of it to which he is born. I think that the children of the clergy sometimes suffer (either by narrowness, or by the reaction from it) from hearing and thinking too much of a clergyman's life.

From a sermon he gave on 'Forbearance':

Who are we, what is our insight into other men's hearts, that we should foreclose the time of their growth; that we should call for speed; when God, it may be, is patiently disengaging their minds from difficulties that we have never known; that we should let ourselves resent their present refusal of the truth, which, perhaps, they are already preparing to welcome later on with a depth, an intensity, a thoroughness of acceptance far beyond all that we have ever rendered to it? If we realize at all the height and greatness of the truth, its hidden depths, its distances of unapproachable light, its divineness and awefulness, we must know ourselves to be incapable of judging how Almighty God may lead men on towards it; we must feel that it would be strange if all men could be led alike, or if we could always tell how others are dealing with their opportunities. God may be leading them by a way that they know not; and they may be humbly, anxiously struggling on; trusting perhaps with a hope they hardly dare put into words, that the light is surely growing somewhat clearer, steadier around them than it was; that they are somehow nearer to God, or at least not further from him than they were . . . Who can measure the responsibility of trying to force on the decision, to presume the issue?

He also wrote the famous prayer:

Almighty God, from whom all thoughts of truth and peace proceed; kindle, we pray Thee, in the hearts of all men the true love of peace, and guide with Thy pure and peaceable wisdom those who take counsel for the nations of the earth: that in tranquillity Thy kingdom may go forward, till the earth be filled with the knowledge of Thy Love: through Jesus Christ our Lord, Amen.

Andrew Cecil Bradley
1851–1935

Bradley, the great Shakespearean critic, was educated at Balliol and then held various university posts before becoming Professor of Poetry at Oxford in 1901. While there, he gave the lectures which formed his important book *Shakespearean Tragedy*, published in 1904. Subsequent Shakespearean criticism may have dissociated itself from some of his methods and conclusions, but no one has doubted the greatness of his contribution.

From a letter of John Bailey to his wife, 3 June 1917:

I had one of the most delightful talks I ever had in my life when Bradley dined on Friday. Like most talk it is impossible to give an account of but we ranged over lots of things . . . and then got into a long talk about religion. I don't know that I got his position very clear – or mine either, indeed! – but while saying that he seldom or never went to Church – because he found the adjustment of the words to his own beliefs too great for habitual use – he quite understood and agreed with the view that, religion being the greatest of all realities and one which no words can state, we do well, if we can, not to forsake the assembling of ourselves together and to use the accepted words with such adjustments as we can. And he himself prays, he told me, and at such times, uses, I gathered, the old words, some or other of them. And he was very strong in pointing out that no thinking man could expect any form of words exactly to express what he individually feels – and therefore in any case even among the orthodox there must be adjustment.

Baron von Hügel
1852–1925

Friedrich von Hügel, the son of an Austrian father and a Scottish mother, spent most of his life in England and became naturalized in 1914. He was the centre of a group of learned Roman Catholics and suffered greatly from the problems and struggles over 'Modernism' in the church in the 1900s – the instructions from Rome as to how far biblical criticism and kindred topics were permissible made some of his friends leave the priesthood, but von Hügel, himself a layman, always remained a devout Catholic. It seems that by 1900 he was already turning more and more to thought and work on prayer, and he was famous as a guide, teacher and help to all who came to him, whether Catholics or others. He had very poor health and was deaf, but overcame these handicaps with great courage.

He wrote:

> . . . *the deeper we get into reality, the more numerous will be the questions we cannot answer. For myself I cannot conceive truth, or rather reality, as a geometrical figure of luminous lines, within which is sheer truth, and outside of which is sheer error; but I have to conceive such reality as light, in its centre blindingly luminous, having rings around it of lesser and lesser light, growing dimmer and dimmer until we are left in utter darkness.*

Bishop Gore
1853–1932

Charles Gore, theologian, Bishop successively of Worcester, Birmingham and Oxford and founder of the Community of the Resurrection, was one of the more alarming characters in the Church of England in the late nineteenth and early twentieth centuries. With his passion for truth, for the betterment of the working classes, for the cause of all underdogs (he denounced the English action of herding Afrikaaner women and children into camps in the Boer War, for example), his faith, his obstinacy and his bristling beard and eyebrows, when he was on the warpath many churchmen in high places must have quailed before him. (There is the famous story of his standing on the bridge over the Thames shaking his fist at Lambeth Palace because some archbishop's compromise had maddened him.) He was one of the group – perhaps the leading member – who published *Lux Mundi* in 1889 and he remained faithful to the view given there that reasonable biblical criticism was not only right but necessary. But in later life he had to give greater emphasis to his other, equally strong view, that to be a clergyman a man must be able to give assent to the two great Creeds. His theological stress was laid on the doctrine of the incarnation and all that flows from it – he had great influence on younger men such as William Temple. On his deathbed, when the Archbishop was visiting him, Gore lapsed into semi-coma, and each time he did so he was heard to say clearly: 'Transcendent glory'.

Bishop Gore once wrote to his friend Bishop Talbot of Winchester:

I am quite sure that our doubters and seekers are much more likely to be won, if they feel clearly what it is we stand for. It is certainly my experience that men who are outside do not come inside without an act of 'repentance', at least intellectual repentance. They come to the end of their own resources. They must 'believe the Gospel'. Let us by all means keep our Gospel free of encumbrances. But let us hold out unflinchingly our essential message.

Dr Scott Lidgett
1854–1953

Almost every cause that might help the people of London was supported by John Scott Lidgett – he founded and was warden of the Bermondsey Settlement in 1891 and remained there throughout his career, he worked for adult education, for better schools, for better conditions for the poor in every way, he was a member of the London County Council, Vice-Chancellor of London University, the editor of a Methodist periodical and the first President of the re-united Methodist Church and only finally retired from work at the age of ninety-five. But his autobiography makes it clear that all this incessant work for others grew from his belief in the guidance of God and the fatherhood of God. He was deeply influenced by F. D. Maurice and Charles Kingsley in thinking that God cares for people's bodies and minds as well as their souls and that we should do so too. He was dissatisfied with the remoteness of God as often described in his youth, and published *The Fatherhood of God in Christian Life and Truth* and *The Spiritual Principle of the Atonement* at the turn of the century, and in his autobiography he described what he was trying to do:

. . . for me at least the decisive fact that both the Prophets of the Old Testament and the Apostles of the New, while insisting that God is 'Other' than man, make it a main object to destroy any sense that He is 'Altogether Other', in order to exhibit His holy perfection as the authoritative standard for men, because 'In Him we live, and move, and have our being'. This is, above all, true of the teaching of Christ. The command 'Be ye therefore perfect, even as your Father in heaven is perfect,' sums up his teaching, and surely bases it upon kinship. The sovereign Kinship of God with men,

126

that is to say His Fatherhood, is the clue by which alike He, they, and the relationships between Him and them must be explained.

A. E. Housman
1859–1936

Alfred Edward Housman was a brilliant Latinist, who produced critical editions of various authors, the most notable being his work on Manilius which he published between 1903 and 1930. In 1892 Housman became Professor of Latin at University College, London, and in 1911 at Cambridge. His first book of poems, *A Shropshire Lad*, dates from 1896 and his *Last Poems* from 1922, though some were printed posthumously. He was a great master of English prose and covered his extreme sensitivity by a severe and alarming exterior, which caused him to become a legend in Cambridge – equally feared and admired.

Easter Hymn

If in that Syrian garden, ages slain,
You sleep, and know not you are dead in vain,
Nor even in dreams behold how dark and bright
Ascends in smoke and fire by day and night
The hate you died to quench and could but fan,
Sleep well and see no morning, son of man.

But if, the grave rent and the stone rolled by,
At the right hand of majesty on high
You sit, and sitting so remember yet
Your tears, your agony and bloody sweat,
Your cross and passion and the life you gave,
Bow hither out of heaven and see and save.

Dean Inge
1860–1954

Dean Inge of St Paul's (commonly called 'The gloomy Dean' because of his refusal to indulge in facile optimism) combined preaching, an active social life, journalism and a deep interest in and much writing and speaking concerning the mystical side of religion, which culminated in his book *Mysticism in Religion* of 1948. He looked to mystical experience rather than belief in the inerrancy of scripture as the verification of religious faith. John Bailey wrote in his diary for 1906:

March 9th. To church at 12. Inge on St John's use of certain words – how he never speaks of faith and knowledge but only of believing and knowing, as if neither process could ever be complete.

In 1912 Dean Inge considered in his own diary the position of liberal churchmen:

I have no doubt that Christianity must cease to depend on belief in miraculous interventions in the order of nature, but I question the wisdom and propriety of such utterances in the pulpit. (He was referring to denials of the Virgin Birth and the physical Resurrection.) Miracle, as Goethe says, is faith's dearest child – the child, not the parent. Traditionalists have a deep sense of loyalty which deserves respect. It is a serious problem for Liberal churchmen, who ought not to conceal their real opinions, but whose duty it is to say what they do, not what they do not believe.

Earl Lloyd George
1863–1945

The Prime Minister, the brilliant politician, the advocate of many Welsh causes, the moving orator and the great radical were all combined in David Lloyd George with a private character of amazing complexity. He can still cause arguments and whoever reads about him becomes confused by the contrasts between the idealist and the opportunist. But under all Lloyd George's subtleties was the child of Welsh Nonconformity (that did not prevent him from describing his countrymen as 'preying on their knees on Sunday and on their neighbours all the rest of the week'); under all the worldliness was the man who cared passionately about the unemployed, the sick and the poor – the man who introduced old-age pensions. He wrote to his brother William, who had lost a son, describing his own feelings when his daughter Mair died, and how it had affected him:

My heart aches for you in your distress. I drank the same cup of sorrow and I know how bitter it is, and words, however sincere, cannot sweeten it. But I should like to tell you this from my own experience. When the blow fell, it all seemed so wantonly cruel . . . I know now what it was for. It gave me a keener appreciation of the sufferings of others. It deepened my sympathy. Little Mair's death has been the inspiration of all my work to relieve human misery during recent years. God alone knows what Mair and my dear nephew – both of them as sweet souls as ever graced this earth – have been saved from by this early flight. I am never sorry for the dead. My grief is all for the living.

Bishop Hensley Henson
1863–1947

The Church of England produces bishops from time to time who belong to no definite party or group, but whose individual personalities are so strong that they almost seem a host in themselves. Bishop Hensley Henson was of this type: when he disagreed with his colleagues – when he disagreed with anyone – he never hesitated to say so. But his great gifts had ample scope as successively Bishop of Hereford and of Durham and in his Ordination Charges to those about to become deacons or priests he gave the best of himself, with immense shrewdness as well as seriousness. His favourite text was 'Jesus Christ the same yesterday, today, yea and for ever'.

In 1924 he wrote to a newly appointed clergyman:

The really essential thing in going into a new parish is to win the trust of the people. It is not so much divergence of habit and point of view that drives a wedge between priest and parishioners as the sense that they have not been dealt with fairly, which the parishioners cannot but have when changes are made which they dislike, the reason of which they do not know or which they misunderstand, and with respect to which no effort was made to gain their approval.

In December 1942 he wrote to a friend:

Don't repeat the error which worked such havoc after the last war, and has not ceased even now to cloud our vision. I mean, the error of seeing pastoral duty in its bearing on 'Youth'. The majority of Christ's sheep will not come under that description: and their problems and difficulties are certainly not less serious than those which disturb adolescent minds. And a too exclusive surrender to the claims and moods of adolescence may diminish the pastor's competence to help those, the majority of his charge, who have left adolescence with its paradoxes and quick changes behind them in their life's journey.

Archbishop Lang
1864–1945

Cosmo Gordon Lang must have been one of the hardest working archbishops of any time, who began his ministerial career as a curate in the slums of Leeds and progressed through the Bishopric of Stepney to York and Canterbury. Some people in his lifetime considered that he was too 'prelatical' – that he enjoyed power and influence too much. (But he was a close friend of George V, who was not noticeably tolerant of pomposity.) Lang was unfairly criticized during the abdication crisis of Edward VIII – in fact he took no part in the proceedings, but he made what was felt to be a tactless broadcast after the King had left England. His biography revealed a man of the deepest spirituality and agonizing humility – he used to go to a remote house in Scotland every year for his holiday and pray in the little oratory he called 'The Cell'. His jottings record how much the quiet meant to him and how he filled the time with prayer and repentance:

In this sacred little place, by God's mercy, watersprings break from a dry and thirsty land. It is a marvel to me that in spite of all my prayerlessness in the busy months of the year, all my forgetfulness of the lessons learnt in the Cell year after year, God does not take His Holy Spirit from me. It is here that my real self – at least what ought to be my real self – lives.

The thought uppermost in my mind when I re-entered the Cell was that of the Prodigal Son. I had been in a far country, too often not ashamed to eat husks fit only for swine. And seldom have I used the old words, 'Father, I have sinned . . . and am no more worthy to be called Thy son,' with more sincerity and shame and great desire for the Father and His House. And once again the wonder was brought back to me of the Father seeing His prodigal a long way off, and running to meet him, and covering him with the robe of forgiveness.

John Bailey
1864–1931

John Bailey's work as a literary critic included such achievements as *Dr Johnson and his Circle*, but he was also a fervent
supporter of the National Trust and did much to help it in its
early days. His *Letters and Diaries* show his sincere faith, but
they also show an almost lifelong preoccupation concerning
the right relation of culture and art to the religion of renuncia-
tion which he found preached in the New Testament.

From a letter of 1915 to Algernon Cecil:

> *I only wanted to say that, on the question of my surprise at your being so
> much occupied with the question of the true Church, we are, as so often
> happens, not using words in the same sense. The quest of truth is often an
> agony for me too: and it is only with great reluctance and very great mental
> discomfort (I might use a stronger word) that I half acquiesce in the
> conclusion that it is not to be attained to here, in so many of its most
> profoundly vital and interesting aspects. What I wondered at was not your
> attaching so much importance to the quest for truth but your view that
> truth is to be found in the authority of any Church, found in one Church
> and not in any other. That attitude seems to me amazing – contrary to all
> history, all probability, to all of what I should call the spirituality of truth's
> nature.*

King George V
1865–1936

The more the history of his reign is studied, the more it is
noticeable how effective the King's uprightness and common-

sense could be at all times of crisis. (He began his reign by a refusal to take an oath whose wording was excessively offensive to his Roman Catholic subjects.) He kept the brisk and matter-of-fact speech he had learnt as a naval officer all his life, and a complete lack of pretentiousness. He was amazed and humbly delighted when his Silver Jubilee showed how his honesty and hard work had endeared him to his people.

Dean Alington had one particular memory of him:

When King George V returned to Windsor after his serious illness, it fell to my lot to preach to him as one of his chaplains. After the service he took me to his study . . . 'I won't say,' said the King, 'that I thought much about prayer when I was at my worst – I was too ill for that; but when I began to get better, I felt I was being held up by the prayers of my people: now I daresay you think that's nonsense!'

— 117 —

Lord Quickswood
1869–1956

Lord Hugh Cecil, fifth son of the Marquess of Salisbury, Queen Victoria's Prime Minister, grew up into a politician of exceedingly vehement views. He was one of the leaders of the more extreme opposition to the Parliament Act of 1911, but his real interests were religious or religio-political. He persistently opposed the law allowing a man to marry his deceased wife's sister and as a member of the Church Assembly he was a terror to bishops. He said exactly what he thought to everyone, including his old friend, Winston Churchill, to whom he was best man. He wrote to Churchill on that occasion:

I earnestly hope that you will be both good and happy married; but remember that Christian marriage is for Christians and cannot be counted on to succeed save for those who are Christians. And the marriage vow must be kept altogether – you cannot merely abstain from adultery and leave loving, cherishing, etc., etc., to go by the board.

He once remarked of his compatriots:

Many people in England think of a church as a kind of spiritual chemist's shop to which one may send for a bottle of religious grace whenever one happens to want it; they have no sense of belonging to an unseen Kingdom with a loyalty to an unseen King.

He was appointed Provost of Eton in 1936, where many famous men trembled before him, and in 1941 was given a peerage by Churchill's wish. In his old age his sight deteriorated badly, and his niece, to whom he had bequeathed his Bible, found a sheet of paper folded inside, on which he had written: 'I finished the parable of the Prodigal Son and this is probably the last thing I shall ever read.'

118

Sir Winston Churchill
1874–1965

In his autobiography *My Early Life* Winston Churchill gave an account of how he first began to read and study when he was a young army officer in India. (Neither of his parents seem to have helped or guided him about religious matters – it had been left to his old nurse and then to his schoolmasters.) He wrote of the time when his intellectual curiosity awoke:

Hitherto I had dutifully accepted everything I had been told . . . I now begin to read a number of books which challenged the whole religious education I had received at Harrow . . . For a time I was indignant at having been told so many untruths, as I then regarded them, by the schoolmasters and clergy who had guided my youth.

Of course if I had been at a University my difficulties might have been resolved by the eminent professors and divines who are gathered there. At any rate, they would have shown me equally convincing books putting the opposite point of view. As it was I passed through a violent and aggressive anti-religious phase which, had it lasted, might easily have made me a nuisance. My poise was restored during the next few years by frequent contact with danger. I found that whatever I might think and argue, I did not hesitate to ask for special protection when about to come under the fire of the enemy: nor to feel sincerely grateful when I got home safe to tea. I even asked for lesser things than not to be killed too soon, and nearly always in these years, and indeed throughout my life, I got what I wanted. This practice seemed perfectly natural, and just as strong and real as the reasoning process which contradicted it so sharply. Moreover the practice was comforting and the reasoning led nowhere. I therefore acted in accordance with my feelings without troubling to square such conduct with the conclusions of thought . . .

It seemed to me that it would be very foolish to discard the reasons of the heart for those of the head. Indeed I could not see why I should not enjoy them both. I did not worry about the inconsistency of thinking one way and believing the other. It seemed good to let the mind explore so far as it could the paths of thought and logic, and also good to pray for help and succour, and be thankful when they came. I could not feel that the Supreme Creator who gave us our minds as well as our souls would be offended if they did not always run smoothly together in double harness. After all He must have foreseen this from the beginning and of course He would understand it all.

Accordingly I have always been surprised to see some of our Bishops and clergy making such heavy weather about reconciling the Bible story with modern scientific and historical knowledge. Why do they want to reconcile them? If you are the recipient of a message which cheers your heart and fortifies your soul, which promises you reunion with those you have loved in a world of larger opportunity and wider sympathies, why should you worry about the shape or colour of the travel-stained envelope; whether it is duly stamped, whether the date on the postmark is right or wrong? These matters may be puzzling, but they are certainly not important. What is important is the message and the benefits to you of receiving it. Close reasoning can conduct one to the precise conclusion that miracles are impossible: that 'it is much more likely that human testimony should err, than that the laws of nature should be violated'; and at the same time one may rejoice to read how Christ turned the water into wine in Cana of Galilee or walked on the lake or rose from the dead. The human brain cannot comprehend infinity, but the discovery of mathematics enables it to be handled quite easily. The idea that nothing is true except what we comprehend is silly, and that ideas which our minds cannot reconcile are mutually destructive, sillier still. Certainly nothing could be more repulsive both to our minds and feelings than the spectacle of thousands of millions of universes – for that is what they say it comes to now – all knocking about together for ever without any rational or good purpose behind them. I therefore adopted quite early in life a system of believing whatever I wanted to believe, while at the same time leaving reason to pursue unfettered whatever paths she was capable of treading.

Evelyn Underhill
1875–1941

A friend and pupil of Baron von Hügel, the famous spiritual director, Evelyn Underhill remained outside the Roman Catholic Church as a fully committed Anglican, with the concurrence of the Baron, himself a Catholic. She was happily married, a lover of art and travel, but increasingly her time was spent in writing on the contemplative life, in taking retreats and in helping people through correspondence. Perhaps her best-known book is *Worship* which was published in 1937, and which dealt with the different forms of Christian adoration. Her letters show that she had a very strong feeling that Christianity demands that everyone's individual relationship with God be respected, stressing the variety of human nature and emphasizing that there can be no stereotyped dealing with human souls.

From a letter of 1911 about keeping Lent:

Personally – in case the idea is of use to you – I have taken to knocking off all aesthetic pleasure in Lent; all poetry, fiction, theatres, music. This I find, at any rate at first, a real deprivation, and absolutely harmless! Also, doing rather dreary social duties one is inclined to shirk and giving up attractive ones.

From a letter of 1937:

All that matters in religion is giving ourselves without reserve to God, and keeping our wills tending towards Him. This we can always do; but to feel devout, fervent, aware of His presence, etc., is beyond our control. Everyone goes through 'dry' times such as you are experiencing. They are of great value as tests of our perseverance, and of the quality of our love; and certainly don't mean that anything is wrong. All lies in how we take them – with patience or with restlessness. As to the experience you describe, thank God for it; but don't worry if you never again have it. Such things do happen to many people from time to time, and especially at the beginning of a new phase in the spiritual life, but in this life such 'awareness' is never continuous and its absence certainly does not necessarily mean that we are stopping it by our own fault. Just be simple and natural with God, ask Him to do with you what He wills, avoid strain and fuss of all kinds, and be careful to keep in charity with all men, and you will have done what is in your power. You say in your letter 'below everything, I believe I'm in a way very quiet and happy' – well, that, not the fluctuating surface moods, represents your true spiritual state, and is the work of God. Give Him thanks for it and trust it and don't bother about the variable weather.

120

Bishop Bell
1883–1958

George Bell, Bishop of Chichester, showed what the office of a bishop can be: he was a Father-in-God not just to the people of his diocese, but to hundreds of others who needed his help. Trained by being chaplain to Archbishop Davidson, he showed successfully as Dean of Canterbury his concern that the arts should be used fully in the service of the church. He wrote Archbishop Davidson's *Life*, which was acclaimed as one of the best biographies in English. When bishop, he was deeply involved in the ecumenical movement, in trying to help the Confessing Church in Germany against the Nazis, in the cause of the refugees in the Second World War and in that of the aliens in England who were interned on suspicion. He protested in the House of Lords against the saturation bombing of civilian targets in Germany, and it has been suggested that by protesting in this way he destroyed his chance of becoming Archbishop of Canterbury on the death of William Temple. He was a friend of the theologian Dietrich Bonhoeffer, who was executed for his resistance to Hitler, and the brief letter given here is the one Bell wrote to him as war came:

My dear Dietrich,
*   You know how deeply I feel for you and yours in this melancholy time.*

*May God comfort and guide you. I think often of our talk in the summer.
May he keep you. Let us pray together by reading the Beatitudes.* Pax Dei
superat omnia nos custodiat.

Yours affectionately,
George.

Dorothy L. Sayers
1893–1957

Famous for her detective stories, and, later, for her translation
of Dante, Dorothy L. Sayers took on a very difficult task when
in 1940 she agreed to write a series of radio plays on the life of
Jesus. When the project was announced, in the autumn of
1941, she had to face a great deal of criticism, and so did the
BBC, for having undertaken such a subject at all; to present the
Gospels in modern speech by a modern playwright being
thought of as a dangerous innovation. When the plays were
given they were exceedingly successful and in the introduction
to the published version Miss Sayers made some interesting
points on the relationship between the four Gospels. Of the
resurrection appearances she wrote:

*The divergences appear very great on first sight; and much ink and
acrimony have been expended on proving that certain of the stories are not
'original' or 'authentic', but are accretions grafted upon the firsthand
reports by the pious imaginations of Christians. Well, it may be so. But the
fact remains that* all *of them, without exception, can be made to fall into
place in a single orderly and coherent narrative without the smallest
contradiction or difficulty, and without any suppression, invention, or
manipulation, beyond a trifling effort to* imagine *the natural behaviour of
a bunch of startled people running about in the dawnlight between
Jerusalem and the Garden.*

C. S. Lewis
1898–1963

C. S. Lewis taught English Literature at Oxford and Cambridge all his adult life, but after his decision in 1931 to rejoin the Church of England he also wrote and broadcast more and more on religious subjects – sometimes by means of novels and children's books, sometimes directly by essays. His books can give the impression of someone who has been too deeply impressed by the mediaeval reverence for logic: he can appear to forget that God is supreme over logic as over all else. His letters reveal another side of him, his immense charitableness and readiness to take pains with individuals.

From a letter of 4 January 1941, to a correspondent who had told him of her decision to become a practising Christian:

Congratulations . . . on your own decision. I don't think this decision comes either too late or too soon. One can't go on thinking it over for ever; and one can begin to try to be a disciple before one is a professed theologian. In fact they tell us, don't they, that in these matters to act on the light one has is almost the only way to more light. Don't be worried about feeling flat, or about feeling at all. As to what to do, I suppose the normal next step, after self-examination, repentance and restitution, is to make your Communion; and then to continue as well as you can, praying as well as you can and fulfilling your daily duties as well as you can. And remember always that religious emotion is only a servant . . . This, I say, would be the obvious course. If you want anything more e.g. Confession and Absolution which our church enjoins on no one but leaves free to all – let me know and I'll find you a directeur. If you choose this way, remember it's not the psychoanalyst over again; the confessor is the representative of Our Lord and declares His forgiveness – his advice or 'understanding' tho' of real, is of secondary importance.

For daily reading I suggest (in small doses) Thomas à Kempis's Imitation of Christ *and the* Theologica Germanica *(Golden Treasury series, Macmillan) and of course the Psalms and NT. Don't worry if your*

heart won't respond; do the best you can. You are certainly under the
guidance of the Holy Ghost, or you wouldn't have come where you now
are; and the love that matters is His for you – yours for Him may at present
exist only in the form of obedience. He will see to the rest.

Archbishop William Temple
1881–1944

William Temple was the son of Frederick Temple, Archbishop
of Canterbury, and through his mother he was directly
descended from the famous Georgiana, Duchess of Devonshire, much of whose charm he seems to have inherited. He
was successively Bishop of Manchester, Archbishop of York
and for two and a half years of war, Archbishop of Canterbury.
He was known as 'the people's Archbishop' because of his
concern for social matters; the causes he supported included
adult education, the ecumenical movement, better treatment
for the unemployed and better housing for slum dwellers. But
he himself always stressed the primacy of prayer, and his
teaching concerning it is profound and demanding. His death,
coming suddenly and unexpectedly, was regretted by all
Christians in England, not just by Anglicans.

Infallible direction for practical action is not to be had either from Bible or
Church or Pope or individual communing with God; and this is not
through any failure of a wise and loving God to supply it, but because in
whatever degree reliance upon such infallible direction comes in, spirit-
uality goes out. Intelligent and responsible judgment is the privilege and
burden of spirit or personality.

Above all, do not spend the whole time of prayer talking yourself. Bring
the needs of the world, and the problems of your life, before God; then leave
them with Him and wait for a while in silence not only from speech, but as
far as possible from thought, just desiring with all your force that in these
things God's will may be done, and resting in the quiet assurance of His
love and power. There is no limit to what God will do by means of us if we
train ourselves to trust Him enough.

SOURCES AND ACKNOWLEDGMENTS

The vast majority of the extracts included come from contemporary documents and are long out of copyright. Some of the pieces are taken from anthologies, some from works which are available in many editions; but when the extract has been discovered in a biography or the like, the relevant details are given so that the reader who is interested in a particular person may enquire further.

1 Bede, *A History of the English Speaking People* translated by Leo Sherley-Price, revised by R. E. Latham, Penguin Classics 1955, 1968; © Leo Sherley-Price 1955, 1968. Used by permission of Penguin Books.

2 The extract from Alfred's work on St Augustine is quoted by Eleanor Duckett in *Alfred the Great*, Collins 1957.

3 From Christopher Brooke, *The Saxon and Norman Kings*, Batsford 1963.

4 The extract from contemporary chronicles is quoted by David C. Douglas in *William the Conqueror*, Eyre Methuen 1964.

5 *The Prayers and Meditations of St Anselm* translated by Sister Benedicta Ward, Penguin Classics 1973; © Benedicta Ward 1973. Used by permission of Penguin Books.

7 The extract from contemporary chronicles is quoted by W. L. Warren in *Henry II*, Methuen 1973.

8 This contemporary account is quoted by Hubert Cole in *The Black Prince*, Granada 1976.

9 Julian of Norwich, *Showings* (*Revelations of Divine Love*) translated by Edmund Colledge OSA and James Walsh SS, Classics of Western Spirituality, Paulist Press and SPCK 1978, p. 253.

10 Geoffrey Chaucer, *The Canterbury Tales* translated by Nevill Coghill, Penguin Classics 1951, 1958, 1960; © Nevill Coghill 1951, 1958, 1960. Used by permission of Penguin Books.

11 *The Book of Margery Kempe* translated by W. Butler-Bowden, Cape 1936, p. 361.

12 The extract from contemporary sources is quoted by E. F. Jacobs in *Henry V and the Invasion of France*, Hodder 1947.

13 *The Paston Letters*, edited and with an introduction by Norman Davis, OUP 1977, p. 151.

14 The quotation from Bishop Fisher can be found in J. R. Lander, *Government and Community: England 1450–1509*, Edward Arnold 1980.

15 The extract from a contemporary document is quoted in Garrett Mattingley, *Catherine of Aragon*, Cape 1942.

16 The extract from a contemporary document is included in *The Lisle Letters* edited by Muriel St Clare Byrne, selected by Bridget Boland, Secker & Warburg 1983.

17 Taken from a modern facsimile of the original letter, which was published in black letter type in 1566 by St John's College.

18 The extract from a contemporary document is quoted by A. G. Dickens in *The English Reformation*, Batsford 1964.

19 The extracts from contemporary documents are quoted by A. E. Pollard in *Thomas Cranmer*, Frank Cass & Co. 1965. The collect is to be found in the Book of Common Prayer.

21 The extract from a contemporary document is quoted by B. W. Beckingsale in *Burghley: Tudor Statesman*, Macmillan 1967.

22 The extract from Jewel's *A Treatise of the Holy Scriptures* is quoted by J. E. Booty in *John Jewel*, SPCK 1963.

23 The document from contemporary sources is quoted by F. S. Boas in *Sir Philip Sidney*, Collins 1955.

24 Edward's prayer is quoted by Hester W. Chapman in *The Last Tudor King*, Cape 1958.

25 Elizabeth's speech is quoted by J. E. Neale in *Elizabeth I and her Parliaments*, Cape 1957.

26 The document from contemporary sources is quoted by Elizabeth Jenkins in *Elizabeth and Leicester*, Gollancz 1961.

27 The document from contemporary sources is quoted by Claire Cross in *The Puritan Earl*, Macmillan 1966.

28 The extracts from contemporary documents are quoted by G. M. Thomson in *Sir Francis Drake*, Secker & Warburg 1972.

29 Raleigh's speech from the scaffold and his poem are quoted by Milton Waldman in *Sir Walter Raleigh*, Collins 1943.

30 The extract from Sidney's *A Work concerning the Trewness of Christian Religion* is quoted by F. S. Boas in *Sir Philip Sidney*, Collins 1955.

31 There have been many editions of Andrewes' *Private Prayers*. I have used *The Preces Privatae of Lancelot Andrewes* edited by A. E. Burn, Methuen 1953.

32 There are various editions and selections of Donne's sermons. This particular extract was quoted by George Bell in his *Life of Randall Davidson*, OUP 1952.

34 Father Augustin Baker, *Holy Wisdom* edited by Rt Revd Abbot Sweeney, Burns & Oates 1911, p. 264.

35 Strafford's letter is quoted by C. V. Wedgwood in *Thomas Wentworth: A Revaluation*, Cape 1961.

38 From *Oliver Cromwell's Letters and Speeches* edited by Thomas Carlyle, Vol. 1, Chapman and Hall 1845.

40 The extracts are quoted in the Introduction to the Everyman edition of Baxter's *Autobiography* edited by J. M. Lloyd Thomas, Dent 1931.

41 From *Memoirs of the Life of Colonel Hutchinson* written by his widow Lucy, Kegan, Paul, Trench, Trubner and Co. 1904.

42 The extract from contemporary sources is included by S. R. Gardiner in *Constitutional Documents of the Puritan Revolution*, OUP 1951.

43 Evelyn's prayer is quoted by Arthur Ponsonby in *John Evelyn*, Heinemann 1933.

44 The extracts are taken from *No More But My Love*, a selection of George Fox's letters edited by Cecil W. Sharman, Quaker Home Service 1980, pp. 116, 117, 131. Used by permission.

45 Lady Temple's letter is quoted by Lord David Cecil in *Two Quiet Lives*, Constable 1948.

47 This account of Charles' death is derived from Antonia Fraser, *King Charles II*, Weidenfeld and Nicolson 1979.

48 Tillotson's letter to the Earl of Shrewsbury is quoted by D. H. Somerville in *The King of Hearts*, Allen and Unwin 1962.

49 Hickes' letter is quoted in the Henry V. Wheatley edition of Samuel Pepys' Diary, 1893–96.

50 The extract from *Advice to a Daughter* is taken from *Halifax: Complete Works* edited by J. P. Kenyon, Penguin 1969.

51 Gilbert Burnet's description is quoted by Vivian de Sola Pinto in *Enthusiast in Wit*, Routledge and Kegan Paul 1962.

52 The extracts from William's writings are quoted by Nesca A. Robb in *William of Orange*, Heinemann 1962.

53 Mrs Burnet, *A Method of Devotion*, Joseph Downing 1713.

54 The extract from a contemporary document is quoted by Marjorie Bowen in *The Third Mary Stuart*, The Bodley Head 1929.

55 *The Journeys of Celia Fiennes* edited by Christopher Morris, The Cresset Press 1947, p. 266.

56 Marlborough's letter is quoted by Winston S. Churchill in his biography *Marlborough*, Vol. 2, Harrap 1947.

58 Butler's sermon is included by H. H. Henson in *Selected English Sermons: Sixteenth to Nineteenth Centuries*, OUP 1939.

59 Wesley's *Prayers for Wednesday Morning* are taken from *John Wesley's Prayers* edited by F. C. Gill, Epworth Press 1951; and his letter to Wilberforce from *The Letters of John Wesley* edited by John Telford, Vol. VIII, Epworth Press 1931.

61 From an edition of *Dr Johnson's Prayers* edited by Elton Trueblood, Prinit Press, Dublin, Indiana 1980.

62 Kitty Witham's letter to her mother is included by Rose Macaulay in *They Went to Portugal*, Cape 1946.

63 Fanny Boscawen's letter is quoted by C. Aspinall-Oglander in *Admiral's Widow*, Hogarth Press 1942.

64 Whitbread's prayer is quoted by Roger Fulford in *Samuel Whitbread*, Macmillan 1967.

65 Pitt's letter to Wilberforce is quoted by Robin Furneaux in *William Wilberforce*, Hamish Hamilton 1974.

68 From *Selected Letters of Sydney Smith* edited by Nowell C. Smith, OUP 1981, p. 94.

70 Lady Anglesey's letter to her husband is quoted by the seventh Marquess of Anglesey in *One-Leg: The Life and Letters of the First Marquess of Anglesey*, Cape 1961.

72 From *The Autobiography of Sir Harry Smith* edited by G. D. Moore-Smith, John Murray 1910, p. 72.

73 From *The Correspondence of Sarah, Lady Lyttelton* edited by the Hon. Mrs Hugh Wyndham, John Murray 1912, p. 412.

74 The extracts from *The Christian Year* and Keble's letter are quoted by Georgina Battiscombe in *John Keble*, Constable 1963.

76 Arnold's prayer is quoted by Dean Stanley in *The Life and Correspondence of Thomas Arnold*, Ward Lock 1890.

78 Lang's words about Newman are quoted by his biographer J. G. Lockhart in *Cosmo Gordon Lang*, Hodder 1949. The extract from J. C. Sharp's *Studies in Poetry and Philosophy* is quoted in a letter of J. J. Hornby included in *Memoirs of Archbishop Temple* by Seven Friends, edited by E. G. Sandford, Macmillan 1906, Vol. 1, p. 91.

79 From *Disraeli's Reminiscences* edited by Helen M. Swartz and Marvin Swartz, Hamish Hamilton 1975, pp. 8, 102.

80 Cobden's letter is quoted by John Morley in *The Life of Richard Cobden*, T. Fisher Unwin 1903.

81 Maurice's letter is quoted by H. G. Wood in *Frederick Denison Maurice*, CUP 1950.

82 Cardinal Vaughan's description of Manning's death was printed in *The Times Literary Supplement* of 24 March 1921.

83 The quotation from and commentary on Gladstone's correspondence with his wife are taken from Georgina Battiscombe, *Mrs Gladstone*, Constable 1956, and are used by permission.

84 Mrs Gaskell's letter to her daughter is quoted by J. A. V. Chapple in *Elizabeth Gaskell: A Portrait in Letters*, Manchester University Press 1980.

85 Bright's letter is quoted by G. M. Trevelyan in *The Life of John Bright*, Constable 1925, from which the second extract is also taken.

86 Tait's prayer is quoted by Randall Davidson in *Archbishop Campbell Tait*, Vol. 1, Macmillan 1891.

87 Church's letter and sermon are quoted by B. A. Smith in *Dean Church*, OUP 1958.

88 Jowett's letters and the reminiscences of Acland and Lang are quoted by Geoffrey Faber in *Jowett*, Faber 1957.

89 From *Letters of the Prince Consort* edited by Dr Kurt Jagon, John Murray 1938, p. 97.

90 From *Letters of Queen Victoria 1837–1861* edited by A. C. Benson and Viscount Esher, John Murray 1907, Vol. 2, p. 336 and Vol. 3, p. 51.

91 Temple's speech is recorded in the Chronicles of Convocation for 11 February 1870 and quoted by E. G. Sandford in *Memoirs of Archbishop Temple* by Seven Friends, Macmillan 1906, Vol. 1, p. 304; and the letter to his son in Vol. 2 of the same work, p. 697.

92 Charlotte Mary Yonge, *Womankind*, Mozeley and Smith 1877, pp. 78f. and 298f.

94 Josephine Butler's speech is quoted by Millicent Fawcett and E. M. Turner in *Josephine Butler*, The Association for Moral and Social Hygiene 1927.

95 The quotation from Dale's sermon is included in A. W. W. Dale, *The Life of R. W. Dale of Birmingham*, Hodder 1898, from which the second extract is also taken.

96 The extracts from Benson's journal are quoted by A. C. Benson in *Edward White Benson*, Macmillan 1901.

97 The extracts from Miss Beale's speech and the letter are quoted by Josephine Kamm in *How Different from Us*, The Bodley Head 1958.

98 The extract from Octavia Hill's writing is quoted by E. Moberly Bell in *Octavia Hill*, Constable 1942.

99 From *The Diary of Lady Frederick Cavendish* edited by John Bailey, John Murray 1927, Vol. 2, pp. 22, 332.

100 Creighton's letters are included by Louise Creighton in *The Life and Letters of Mandell Creighton*, Longmans Green & Co. 1904, Vols. 1 and 2.

101 Talbot's letter is quoted by Gwendolen Stephenson in *Edward Stuart Talbot*, SPCK 1936.

102 Rosebery's letter is quoted by Robert Rhodes James in *Rosebery*, Weidenfeld and Nicolson 1963.

103 Illingworth's letter is included by A. L. Illingworth in *The Life and Work of John Richard Illingworth*, John Murray 1917.

104 Davidson's sermon is quoted by Bishop George Bell in his biography *Randall Davidson*, OUP 1952.

105 Paget's letter, sermon and prayer are quoted by S. Paget and J. M. C. Crum in *Francis Paget, Bishop of Oxford*, Macmillan 1912.

106 From *John Bailey 1864–1931: Letters and Diaries* edited by Sarah Bailey, John Murray 1935, p. 179.

107 Friedrich von Hügel, *The Reality of God and Religion and Agnosticism*, Dent 1931.

108 Bishop Gore's letter is quoted by G. L. Prestige in *The Life of Charles Gore*, Heinemann 1935.

109 J. Scott Lidgett, *My Guided Life*, Methuen 1936, pp. 153f.

110 'Easter Hymn', *Collected Poems of A. E. Housman*, Cape and Holt Rinehart & Winston, NY, 1939.

111 W. R. Inge, *Diary of a Dean: St Pauls 1911–1934*, Hutchinson 1949, p. 14.

112 Lloyd George's letter is quoted by John W. Derry in *The Radical Tradition*, Macmillan 1967.

113 From *Letters of Herbert Hensley Henson* edited by E. F. Braley, SPCK 1950, pp. 31, 238.

114 The extracts from Lang's notebooks are quoted by his biographer J. C. Lockhart in *Cosmo Gordon Lang*, Hodder 1949, pp. 187ff.

115 From *John Bailey 1864–1931: Letters and Diaries* edited by Sarah Bailey, John Murray 1935, p. 154.

116 From C. A. Alington, *A Dean's Apology*, Faber 1952, pp. 170f.

117 The extract from Cecil's letter to Churchill of 5 September 1908 and the other comments are quoted by Kenneth Rose in *The Later Cecils*, Weidenfeld and Nicolson 1975.

118 W. S. Churchill, *My Early Life*, Thornton Butterworth 1930, pp. 127–31.

119 From *The Letters of Evelyn Underhill* edited by Charles Williams, Longmans Green & Co. 1943, pp. 124, 261.

120 Bell's letter to Bonhoeffer is quoted by his biographer Ronald Jasper in *George Bell: Bishop of Chichester*, OUP 1967.

121 Dorothy L. Sayers, *The Man Born to be King*, Gollancz 1943, p. 35.

122 *Letters of C. S. Lewis* edited by W. H. Lewis, Geoffrey Bles 1966, p. 191.

123 The extracts are taken from William Temple, *Nature, Man and God*, Macmillan 1934, p. 353; and the *Manchester Diocesan Magazine* of February 1925.